Situated Writing as Theory and Method

This creative and original book develops a framework for situated writing as theory and method, and presents a trilogy of untimely academic novellas as exemplars of the uses of situated writing.

It is an inter- and trans-disciplinary book in which a diversity of forms are used to create a set of interwoven novellas, inspired by poststructuralist and postcolonial feminist theory and literary fiction, along with narrative life writing genres such as diaries and letters, memory work, poetic writing, and photography. The book makes use of a politics of location, situated knowledges, diffraction, and intersectionality theories to promote situated writing as a theory and method for exploring the complexity of social life through gender, whiteness, class, and spatial location.

It addresses writing as an inter- and trans-disciplinary form of scholarship in its own right, with emancipatory potential, emphasising the role of writing in shaping creative, critical, and reflexive approaches to research, education, and professional practice. It is useful for researchers, teachers, postgraduate and PhD students in feminist and intersectionality studies, narrative studies, and pursuing interdisciplinary approaches across the humanities, social sciences, design, and the arts to inspire a theory and method for situated writing.

Mona Livholts, PhD, is an Associate Professor of Social Work in the Department of Culture and Social Studies, Linköping University, Sweden; founder of The Network for Reflexive Academic Writing Methodologies (RAW) 2008–2017. Her research focuses on emergent writing methodologies in a wider context of method transformation saturated by gender-, inter- and transdisciplinarity, creative, and art-based methods, in particular auto/biographical and narrative life writing genres such as diaries and letters, memory work, poetry, and photography. Research themes include media narratives on rape, gender, space and communication, and glocalised social work. Books include: *Emergent Writing Methodologies in Feminist Studies* (2012), *Discourse and Narrative Methods: Theoretical Departures, Analytical Strategies and Situated Writing* (with Tamboukou 2015), and *Social Work in a Glocalised World* (with Bryant 2017).

Routledge Advances in Research Methods

Action Research in Policy Analysis
Critical and Relational Approaches to Sustainability Transitions
Edited by Koen P.R. Bartels and Julia M. Wittmayer

Doing Public Ethnography
How to Create and Disseminate Ethnographic and Qualitative
Research to Wide Audiences
Phillip Vannini

Reflexivity
Theory, Method and Practice
Karen Lumsden (with Jan Bradford and Jackie Goode)

Dialectics, Power, and Knowledge Construction in Qualitative Research
Beyond Dichotomy
Adital Ben-Ari and Guy Enosh

Researching Social Problems
Edited by Amir Marvasti and A. Javier Treviño

Action Research in a Relational Perspective
Dialogue, Reflexivity, Power and Ethics
Edited by Lone Hersted, Ottar Ness and Søren Frimann

Situated Writing as Theory and Method
The Untimely Academic Novella
Mona Livholts

For more information about this series, please visit: www.routledge.com/Routledge-Advances-in-Research-Methods/book-series/RARM

Situated Writing as Theory and Method
The Untimely Academic Novella

Mona Livholts
Foreword by Liz Stanley

Routledge
Taylor & Francis Group

LONDON AND NEW YORK

First published 2020
by Routledge
2 Park Square, Milton Park, Abingdon, Oxon OX14 4RN

and by Routledge
52 Vanderbilt Avenue, New York, NY 10017

Routledge is an imprint of the Taylor & Francis Group, an informa business

British Library Cataloguing-in-Publication Data
A catalogue record for this book is available from the British Library

Library of Congress Cataloging-in-Publication Data
A catalog record has been requested for this book

ISBN: 978-0-367-27602-7 (hbk)
ISBN: 978-0-429-29683-3 (ebk)

Typeset in Times New Roman
by codeMantra

MIX
Paper from
responsible sources
FSC   FSC® C013985
www.fsc.org

Printed in the United Kingdom
by Henry Ling Limited

Contents

Tables and figures

Table

Figures

Foreword

Situated writing, authorship and readership

Liz Stanley

University of Edinburgh

The title – *Situated Writing as Theory and Method* – and the sub-title – *The Untimely Academic Novella* – of Mona Livholts's most welcome book are equally important, for each informs the other. 'Situated writing', the focus of Part I, is a zeitgeist idea made material around articulating the practices involved in producing the untimely (what is out of, or in another, time and space), academic (the working context or location), novellas (short writings that combine fact and fiction about a constructed persona that the author inscribes as though themselves). Situated writing is therefore to be seen as a form of reflexive autobiography mixed with story-telling which exemplifies as well as promotes its claims in terms of situated knowledge (drawing here on Donna Haraway) as represented through this situated writing. The three untimely academic novellas, forming Part II, are crucial in this: they are the method by which the theory is demonstrated. Together, theory and method characterise both Part I *and* Part II, rather than being divided between them. They combine to show the import of the politics of location and that all representations come from a point of view. And they also demonstrate the import of the politics of translation, both in a literal sense, from one language to another, and in a figurative sense, from the spoken or visual to the written, and from the factional to the fictoid.

The role of these introductory comments about situated writing and the untimely novellas is to provide a foreword to this book. However, readers might ask, what exactly is a foreword, and how does it relate to a preface? Typically, the writer of a foreword is invited by an author or a publisher or both to write something in general terms about the character of the book that follows – in a literal sense, it is a '(be)fore-word'. Also typically, the writer of a preface is the author and they use it to 'pre-face', to stand in front of, their book by situating in specific terms some particular aspect/s of it. Both come before the main text, though they are by different people, serve different purposes, and have different genre conventions, like a foreword is signed, but who writes a preface is subsumed in the main authorial name. But still, both directly address the reader, both are short, both come before, both are intended to serve useful purposes by giving the reader some (general/ specific) material additional to what is in the main text. Consequently, while distinguishing between them might seem unimportant, doing so raises important questions about *authorship* and that different authors of different components of the text being read have been at work, and also some equally important questions about *readership*.

What is being indicated through considering the foreword and preface distinction is that, while the hand/keyboard/voice recognition software that writes may be singular, there are complexities and multiplicities involved. These are the many complexities that are analysed through the theory and practice of situated writing, and which are the central concern of this book. Succinctly, a foreword and a preface are both, but differently, located in a context that has strong 'chronotopic' aspects in which, as Mikhail Bakhtin puts it, different space and time configurations intersect, those of different readings as well as of different writings. Different readings? Yes, those of the multiple readers of published books, but also the singular reader who is the person who reads an unpublished manuscript in order to write a foreword for a later published version, and later on the different kind of reading provided by a copy-editor. And different writings? Yes, including the writing by the author, the writing of the foreword-provider, and the writing of publishers in providing synopses and other copy used to promote the book.

Added to this, there are the other readings and writings that also underpin the content of a book that is written and prefaced by an author and given a foreword by an interested third-party. They are those that belong to the slice of life that a book is 'about', and also those that inhere in the writing process that the author engages in when shaping – sculpting – its contents in the ways they have, using the rhetorical and other devices they have. A book of whatever kind is a 'heterotopia', a Maurice Blanchot and Michel Foucault term for a created small world with its own characters, rules, regulations, prevailing truths and lies, behaviours, plot-lines, beginnings and endings. This is to invoke genre while also recognising that pure types (fact, fiction, science, autobiography, novel) rarely exist and that the ontological parameters of these forms of writing are usually to one degree or another permeable. Authors are, after all, human and creatively active, although contemporary theoretical orthodoxies may imply otherwise. And relatedly, a book that results from such complexities is necessarily marked by aspects of its referential origins (the 'who, what, where, when, why' aspects) as well as its authorial inscription (the 'how' aspects). Books are complicated, and can be read as well is written in a wide variety of ways.

But *why* a foreword to a book, what is its purpose? These are usually written by interested third-parties who are known to be knowledgeable but who also have a degree of independence, with the contents therefore seen as likely to be measured and having credibility. The purpose of a foreword, then, is at basis to give added authority to the book in question. In this context, and as commented in this book's acknowledgements, I was party to the untimely novellas being given in a number of academic contexts, as an interesting and innovative form of writing and greatly to be supported. The subsequent introduction of the RAW (Reflexive Academic Writing) Network and its activities and a related book by Mona Livholts and Maria Tamboukou (2015), *Discourse and Narrative Methods*, added methodological substance, with *Situated Writing as Theory and Method* providing yet further substantial theoretical *and* practical developments of this innovative and sustained intellectual project. At the same time, my own work has taken me in different conceptual and methodological directions, into theorising auto/biography, documents of life, and epistolary theory, and also into developing a more philosophical version of analytical reflexivity. Some strategic differences result, to which there are no incontrovertible solutions, but which show that a range of different responses can be encompassed within very similar approaches.

Ideas about the 'death of the author', initially associated with poststructuralism and the work of Michel Foucault and Roland Barthes, have now become a kind of conceptual orthodoxy rather than an insight for debate. They are discussed in this book in a nuanced way in seeing authors as working within intertextual connections and genre constraints but still exerting authority over the products of writing. Relatedly, situated writing by definition centres an extremely active author involved in fashioning and self-fashioning when writing a text. The author here is alive, active, innovative, opinionated, and very interesting. The resulting tensions are handled through exploring in some depth the material basis of writing and the persona it fashions, provoking the reader to engage with its arguments and to explore their configurations in the untimely novellas in Part I as well as in the chapters in Part I.

In this connection, while recognising the same issues and experiencing the same tensions, my own approach has been to focus on both the active reader *and* the active writer/editor. Doing so has involved a series of grounded projects investigating the practices involved in reading circulating texts such as letters and other 'documents of life' in their original contexts of reading, the 'epistolary pact' and its complications, the practices of re-reading 'slantwise' against the grain of textual intention, cultural assemblage as a process by which both everyday and other collections of texts are produced and used. This adds up to a complimentary rather than oppositional approach to the one developed in this book, for there are no clear right or wrong responses to the crucial issues surrounding authorship and readership, and it is important that experimentation, innovation, and new developments continue to occur and are debated.

Reflexivity is another, related, conceptual idea that has taken on connotations of orthodoxy, that all good research must be reflexive. However, what this reflective aspect consists of can encompass many different things. The situated writing approach to this is fully consonant with its helpfully delineated aims and objectives, and focuses on the practices involved in situated writing concerned with producing a complicated form of autobiography that centres self in its relational context, including through the mechanism of an authorial persona. Here, reflexivity is a major tool in explicating both the relational context and the processes of interiority of this constructed factual/fictive persona, with the three untimely novellas in Part II providing detailed expositions of the kinds of practices involved.

However, analytical reflexivity has been central to my own work from the later 1970s on, though this has been articulated in a different way from the reflexivity of situated writing. For me, the analyst is a tool rather than an autobiographical focus, regarding how understanding develops and interpretations are made of whatever grounded contexts and bodies of data are of research concern. Analytical reflexivity in this sense has been influenced by ordinary language philosophy and can be as readily operationalised in relation to analysing a large numerical datasets as to a group of letters, a diary, or the researcher's own notes and commentaries. It is not autobiographical in the usual sense, self in that personal sense is not part of the frame. Among other things, its point is to produce grounded and fully defensible knowledge-claims that can be traced back to a body of material and how this might be read and understood. However, situated writing has at its heart working in a very grounded way and opening up to readers the processes that have brought about a set of circumstances, again with the three untimely novellas providing the clearest indication of how reflexivity features in a situated writing approach. Here my approach and the one developed in this book can be seen to be related and with these differences coexisting with similarities and shared concerns.

The three untimely academic novellas have been mentioned at a number of points, and this foreword concludes by returning to their important role in the production of the body of theory and method that constitutes situated writing. The point made at the start needs reiterating here: the reader will find theory and method in Part I, and will also find both theory and method in Part II. It is not a matter of the theory being in the posh academic work in Part I, and the method bring the practical fictionalised writing in the more immediately accessible Part II! Of course they are different, they make different kinds of claims on the reader and encourage different strategies for readership, as well as being presented in different authorial voices. Equally of course, that is the point of situated writing. Situated writing recognises and is responsive to different contexts, both of writing and of reading. It has become an important presence on the academic scene, it engages readers in a very direct way, and its position will be confirmed and enhanced by this most interesting book. Read on!

Preface

Notes on becoming an untimely academic novelist

'If you don't feel scared when you write a book, then don't write it', my academic friend says to me. We are sitting over coffees at a table in her room at the university. The subject of our conversation, and shared passion, is writing. It is early May 2017, and I have just arrived in the South East of England for a sabbatical period to write this book. Her encouraging and comforting words are a response to my thoughts about my feeling that writing this book is risky and that it makes me feel vulnerable, an experience which has been particularly stressful during the last few years.

I have made use of autobiographical, narrative, life-writing genres and photography to textually and visually illustrate the shaping of my personal history and scholarly identity over almost two decades. The trilogy of untimely academic novellas in this book, which are used as exemplars in creating a framework for situated writing as theory and method, are perhaps best described as novellas about a woman academic who writes about her struggles with writing and the gendered relations of power in the social sciences and beyond. In turn, this influences her career in unexpected ways, but also her life and the lives of those she cares about and loves. The writing of this book resonates with Gannon's (2012: 7) description of how writing in the becoming of academic was experienced as 'haunted by a sense of loss, [...] experienced as a series of tiny aphronias, blocks, stoppages, impossibilities'. The 'I' and 'she' in the untimely academic novellas are also the 'I' and 'me' in this writing moment, and working with this book created movements in the intersections of memory fragments, correspondences, and photographic acts. In the process of rereading and editing the novellas for this book, I have been haunted by the main character, with the name 'woman', her struggles, resistance, privileges, failures, and passion for writing while trying to obtain a professor's chair in the discipline of social work at the beginning of the 21st century in Sweden.

The conceptual framework of the untimely academic novella is created from a set of theoretical ideas and methodological strategies that illustrate situated writing. 'Untimely' allows the writer to speak from a position out of time, a space in the margins, a writing position that acknowledges a complex view of social change through the lag and delay of misunderstandings and misconceptions and through social relations of power and social change; 'academic' because the narrator's main site of writing is academia, the novellas are set in a university and published in scientific journals and books; they are 'novellas' because they borrow inspiration from feminist literary fiction, the novella and the theatre, to create scene and architecture, characters, tone, and style. Thus, the becoming of an untimely academic novella writer and the writing of this book actualise a number of disjunctions that I believe Jolly (2011) describes so well in her analysis of the field of critical and creative life writing, as a field of mutable genres where tensions arise. The last novella in the trilogy, 'Writing Water' (Livholts 2013), illustrates this by making use of the poetic and visual language of water to represent the dissolvability of disciplinary boundaries, which, instead of a professor's chair, opens up possibilities for a multitude of futures. In this book, writing about a professor's chair, snow angels, and the turbulences and stillness of water signals the importance of considering the environmental sustainability of universities as equal and safe spaces to work and write.

This project has transformed alongside changing social relations and conversations, unexpected encounters and struggles, and I am reminded of how the writing and publishing of any book is intimately linked with temporality and spatiality, university politics, and publishing culture. Indeed, the book itself has become a specific materialised, real, and imaginative lived space saturated by delays and, not least, a book that demonstrates what I would call slow writing. As hooks (1989: 145) wrote, it is necessary to have time to write, and time to 'wait through silences'. I find it to be of vital importance that the grant I received from a Swedish research council to write this book made it visible how, for so long, I had perceived it as impossible and embarrassing scholarship, how it had been surrounded by silence, or oddness, in my daily work at the university and how it disqualified my merits as a researcher within the discipline of social work in a Swedish context. I think this is an experience to learn from. How is it possible to accommodate waiting through silences and not lay aside, reject, or destroy one's writing? This makes me think about Piper's (1993) argument that she does not believe that the necessary process of thinking clearly about one's own work is possible if it finds no recognition and remains invisible within the context in which it is based. This in turn, she warns, can create ignorance on the part of the writer towards their own creative contributions. For me, slow writing has emerged as a response to such conditions. The ontology of slow writing, which resonates with the striving for sustainable futures of writing, has been taken up by Ulmer (2017) to acknowledge a slower form of scholarly being, as reflected through writing; a being that is confirmatory of interruptions and allows for sensory writing, and the materiality of the localities of the writer.

I hope that this book will find a place in this time. The writing has been ongoing for more than a decade, and its historical context is substantially longer. The plot that runs across the novellas concerns a woman academic who writes about her struggles with writing in the context of institutional academic hierarchies, disciplinary divides, and borders. It does not set out to be a single true account of what women as a collective encounter in academia. Instead, I suggest that it can be read as a consequence of writing a life, of what it can mean to be named 'woman' and how living a life that challenges the concept of what a professor is, situates and resituates the writing subject. It is within the pluralities and always contextual within the society in which we live that gender is a process of becoming. Additionally, in this project, the life of the writer is also shaped by whiteness and class, by local sites, landscapes, and weather conditions. As I finish the project, ageing is making itself known as patterns of wrinkles, making new imprints on my body, and my self, in this society and in academia. I know what a glass ceiling is. Because it is called a glass ceiling, we who are subjected to its repressive force are not expected to talk about the pain it inflicts. I find Ahmed's (2017: 10) words insightful and helpful as she writes: 'Think of this: how we learn about worlds when they do not accommodate us [...] of the kind of experiences you have when you are not expected to be there'. The contemporary #MeToo movement, that enabled so many women to publish their stories as a resistance to sexualised violence and power abuse, has created a movement for gender equality and changes in university cultures (Bondestam & Lundqvist 2018). By this, I don't mean to suggest that #MeToo is representative of all women (Zarkow & Davies 2018). Neither does this book claims to generalise the situation for women in academia, in Sweden or elsewhere. However, within the architectural, cultural, and institutional academic spaces, language, words and texts, bodies, rooms, and powers give shape to knowledge, disciplines, and inequalities in the lives of writing subjects as gendered, classed, and racialised beings. Documentation never stays on the page, but is intimately intertwined with the author's lived endeavours. Situated writing takes shape through narrative life writing genres and is complex, difficult, multivocal, creative, and sensory. If written stories are untimely, the writing may be characterised by delays, and the author is bound to continue to write. This is what I have unwillingly experienced. I hope that my slow writing has been untimely for long enough and that the book will inspire readers and writers in academia and beyond to promote situated writing within equal and safe university spaces.

Acknowledgements

Thank you to Liz Stanley, Professor of Sociology and ESRC Professorial Research Fellow, Sociology, School of Social and Political Science, Edinburgh University, UK. Without the support I received from you and from the inspiring seminars at The Centre for Narrative and Auto/Biographical Studies that you arranged, the writing and publishing of this trilogy of untimely academic novellas in English would not have been possible. Thank you also to Professor Maria Tamboukou and The Centre for Narrative Research, University of East London, who supported my work with the untimely academic novellas and with whom I co-authored a book in which situated writing was first developed.

Thank you to The Swedish Foundation for Humanities and Social Sciences for financing a sabbatical period during spring 2017, which made writing this book possible. During that sabbatical, the School of Education and Social Work and the Centre for Innovation in Social Work Research, University of Sussex, constituted a welcoming and inspiring space to think and write. Thank you to Angela Wigglesworth at Castle Banks in Lewes for providing wonderful accommodation and inspiring conversations during my sabbatical and for proof-reading the novellas.

Emily Briggs, commissioning editor at Routledge Focus, thank you for professional guidance and for believing in this book to find its readers. Thank you also to the anonymous reviewers for your time to read and provide constructive feedback on the book proposal, and to Liz Sourbout, for excellent language editing.

Part II of this book includes a trilogy of untimely academic novellas that were previously published in the form of two journal articles and a chapter in an edited volume. These have gone through minor editorial revisions for the purpose of being re-published as exemplars of novellas in this monograph. I am grateful to the publishers for their permission to reprint the following material:

Livholts, Mona (2010a) The Professor's Chair: An Untimely Academic Novella. *Life Writing* 7(2), August: 155–168. Commentaries on The Professor's Chair: Erla Hulda Haldorsdottir, Matti Hyvärinen, Kali Israel, Stevi Jackson, Barbara A. Mitzal, Andrea Salter, Liz Stanley, Maria Tamboukou. The first part of the article, pages 156–164, is reprinted with permission from Routledge, Taylor and Francis. Copyright © 2010.

Livholts, Mona (2010b) The Snow Angel and Other Imprints: An Untimely Academic Novella. *International Review of Qualitative Research* 3(1), May 2010: 103–124. The first part of the article, pages 104–118, is reprinted with permission from UC Press. Copyright © 2010.

Livholts, Mona (2013) Writing Water: An Untimely Academic Novella. In: Stanley, Liz (Ed.), *Documents of Life Revisited: Narrative and Biographical Methods for a 21st Century of Critical Humanism*. Farnham: Ashgate. The first part of the chapter, pages 177–187, is reprinted with permission from the publisher of 'Writing water: an untimely academic novella', in *Documents of Life Revisited* edited by Liz Stanley (Farnham: Ashgate, 2013), pp. 177–192. Copyright © 2013.

Aim and organisation of this book

Emergent genres of narrative life writing can be localised in the intersection of feminist and postcolonial studies, human and social sciences, and across the arts. This book develops a genre-transgressive textual and visual strategy that is useful for exploring shifting and diverse contexts and conditions, a form of auto/biographical narrative guided by the idea of research as a creative, critical, and reflexive story-telling practice. The book includes exemplars from my trilogy of untimely academic novellas: 'The Professor's Chair' (Livholts 2010a), 'The Snow Angel and Other Imprints' (Livholts 2010b), and 'Writing Water' (Livholts 2013). The common features of untimely academic novella writing are its critical, creative, and reflexive approach to constructing academic textuality beyond the author, and to elaborating possible forms of the symbolic, visual, and sensory in research. The plot of the novellas unfolds within the university; the writing happens both in the process of writing by the author, and for the main character in the novella in other places. This representational form of analytical reflexivity engages the situated researcher to work from diffracted locations and to engage with the conceptual, emotional, material, and political practices of research.

The overall aim of this book is to develop the contribution of narrative life writing genres to promote situated writing as a framework for creative, critical, and reflexive practices in research and education, and to publish a trilogy of untimely academic novellas.

More specifically, the main themes and objectives are to:

*   develop situated writing as theory and method to promote creative, critical, and reflexive practice in research and education.
*   address issues of writing research related to authorship, privilege, and subjugated knowledge.

- connect the social act of writing and the conditions of writing with the shaping of life stories, the researcher, and the work.
- present and apply diverse textual and visual strategies in auto/biography and life writing, such as diaries, letters, memories, poetry, and photography.
- develop a complex notion of intersectional relations of power by using a variety of writing styles and visual production.
- deepen knowledge about the novella form as a genre-transgressive textual and visual strategy.

How to situate and read this book

This book is shaped as an inter- and trans-disciplinary work, reaching out to readers in the fields of feminist and intersectionality studies, narrative studies, and across the humanities, social sciences, design, and the arts. The book can be read in different ways and selectively, depending on the reader's interest and preferences. One reading strategy is to begin with the theory and method section on situated writing in Part I. This may appeal to readers with an interest in gaining insight into the theoretical inspiration from feminist theorising and narrative life writing genres that shapes the composition of the novellas. Another reading strategy is to begin with the trilogy of novellas in Part II as exemplars that illustrate diverse forms of narrative life writing, which give shape to the framework of situated writing in Part I.

From Part I, readers can choose the sections about which they feel most interested in gaining more in-depth knowledge. The first chapter presents situated knowledge, diffraction, and situated intersectionality to explain how one can deepen the understanding of limited knowledge claims, diffractive story-telling, ways of seeing, analytical reflexivity, and relations of power. The second chapter can be read selectively and reread in regard to the interest in diverse narrative life writing genres, such as memory work, writing diaries and letters, poetry, and photography, depending on the reader's main interest. Both chapters in Part I begin with a broader introduction to the specific theoretical concepts and method practices they address.

In Part II, each of the novellas constitutes a separate piece that can be read independently of the others. Each novella begins with an abstract to guide the reading. As a life writing project, the trilogy invites the reader into a fragmented and seasonal non-linear narration that works from the site of the body, and at the same time beyond the human embodied self, seeking dialogue with the furniture of a professor's chair, with shifting materials and landscapes through snow and water, experimental snow angel writing, and writing through the turbulences and stillness of water.

Part II concludes with a set of open questions and concerns for readers who are seeking inspiration for their own combination of situated writing.

Part I

Situated writing as theory and method

1   The whys and hows of situated writing as theory and method

Why was this book written? What previous writings made it possible, and what are the main points of departure for situated writing as theory and method? In the introduction to the edited book, *Emergent Writing Methodologies in Feminist Studies* (Livholts 2012a: 1), I write that it seems timely that it is published during springwinter, *vårvinter*,[1] a seasonal shift in the geographical space of the mid-Sweden area that blurs the contours of two established seasons, winter and spring. I thought of this as an in-between-ness that also characterised the contribution of that book, written by members of the network for Reflexive Academic Writing (RAW) that I founded and led during the years 2008–2017. My own experiences of being untimely/out of place in academic life led me to create that space for collaboration, performances, and networking, together with academics, professionals, and activists. In line with Richardson's (1994: 927) argument: 'How we are expected to write affects what we can write about', I argued that creativity and analytical reflexivity fall flat under the pen of the dry, distanced author in research and academic writing. The potential to create new knowledge that opens up space for multiple voices, that opens up opportunities for diversity and promoting critical and analytical reflexivity, is greater if diverse languages and genres are brought into use. In the RAW network, we connected voicing, narration, gender and intersections of power with writing as an inventive force to promote sustainable academic futures. I conceptualise the reshaping of knowledge as *post/academic writing*, characterised by inclusivity, untimeliness, and intersectionality (Livholts 2008, 2012a, 2012b; see also Livholts 2009).

The term *situated writing* was first introduced in the book *Discourse and Narrative Methods* where we, Livholts and Tamboukou (2015: 194–195), defined it as '[...] a methodological strategy that combines feminist theorising of situated knowledges (Haraway 1988) and writing as a methodological tool (Livholts 2012)'. Thus, we proposed that situated writing is grounded in feminist philosophies and theories of situated knowledges, but replaced the concept of knowledge with writing to encourage a diversity of ways to theorise and practise methods of situated writing. We argued that diffraction is very useful as a strategy to promote reflexivity, and in Part III of our book, we write about how diaries and letters, memories and images, and the untimely academic novella are all useful as forms of situated writing. Against this background, this book *Situated Writing as Theory and Method: The Untimely Academic Novella* is both a forerunner and a successor to *Emergent Writing Methodologies in Feminist Studies* (Livholts 2012) and *Discourse and Narrative Methods: Theoretical Departures, Analytical Strategies and Situated Writing* (Livholts & Tamboukou 2015).

Questions relating to theory are important in relation to writing, because the transformative power of textual shaping tends to actualise a critique of what 'counts' as (feminist) theory (hooks 1989; Stanley & Wise 2000; Grosz 2010; Ahmed 2017). In the above-mentioned book (Livholts 2012a: 6), I argued for the importance of acknowledging: 'the intimate relationship between academic life and writing as a practice that theorizes and promotes agency and an ethics for change'. Feminist and postcolonial writers have paved the way for a field of writing in which theorising is embodied and writing is formative and border-crossing, emotional, analytically reflective, and open to a multitude of stories (Anzaldúa 1987; Williams 1991; hooks 1997; Richardson 1997; Lykke 2014; Gordon 2015; Ahmed 2017). In her book *Living a Feminist Life*, Ahmed (2017: 7) suggests that we should think about feminist theory as 'homework'. She argues that theory is not primarily created in the academy and says: 'I want to suggest that feminist theory is something we do at home'. The experiences of living a feminist life and theory are intertwined, which means that theorising happens in many different places and relations, at a kitchen table, at a meeting, or in a seminar room. As I show through my untimely academic novellas, situated writing is an artistic practice that takes artefacts as pieces of text as well as visual images, creating mo(ve)ments for change through writing the professor's chair, the snow angel, and water (cf. Livholts 2018). Ahmed (2017: 3) elaborates upon feminism as movement and writes: 'We are moved to become feminists' and 'Many feminisms mean many movements'. Furthermore, these movements take the shape of water:

> I think of feminist action as like ripples in water, a small wave, possibly created by agitation from weather; here, there, each movement making another possible, another ripple, outward, reaching.

In this book, I suggest that we regard theory as homework and as mo(ve) ment; thought, sensed, and practised, through theoretical lenses of situatedness and the diversity of genre forms that narrative life writing offers. Acts of writing and visual images materialise scenes from embodied lives through the writing of memories, poems, letters, diaries, and photography.

A theory and method for situated writing acknowledges the formative character and force of all writing, and resists labelling some writing as alternative or different. To become situated writers, we need to include the whys and hows of writing as part of our practices as engaged researchers and educators. As Coylar (2009: 421) argues, '"Why we write" is not often part of our scholarly conversations'. In the book *Why I Write*, Orwell (1946/2004: 5) suggests that early influences on writing may have something interesting to tell us and that there are all kinds of reasons for writing. These can include egoism, enthusiasm, aesthetic force, sound, beauty, rhythm, a historical impulse of interest in specific events, and a political purpose to 'push the world in a certain direction'. Situated writers bring with them glimpses of the writers' rooms and say something about the history, conditions, possibilities and difficulties, the institutional cultures of writing, and the limitations and transgressions that they have faced. With increasing awareness about why we write, we can locate and re-locate the diversity of experiences and forces for writing. Situated writers transgress the science/academic/ literary/fiction divides and seek to learn from writers across genres about what writing means to them, about the practices and aesthetics of writing. In a series of public and personal conversations on writing with academic scholars in the fields of gender studies and social work, I learned that writing is contextual, procedural, material, imaginative, hard labour, passionate, and geopolitically framed (Livholts 2009, 2010c).

Situated writers are part of a movement for sustainable futures characterised by creative, dialogical, reflexive, safe, and equal spaces where the research(er) is situated – located, seated, placed, positioned – in mo(ve)ment. I have argued (Livholts 2013: 189) that it is important 'to employ a situated and passionate writing to awaken the senses and emotions of readers, to "touch" the reader and create engagement for change'. The page is the space where the eye and the vision meet the hands and the words, not merely literally, but also materially and socially in the context of historical memory and contemporary society (Livholts 2018). Neither the writer nor the reader comes to the page with nothing from nothing. In the book

On Writing (2000: 106), King writes that 'you must not come lightly to the blank page' and makes use of the expression 'creative sleep' as a metaphor (King 2000: 156) for writing. Creative sleep illustrates that both writing and sleeping are physical acts 'encouraging our minds to unlock from the humdrum of rational thinking of our daily lives' (ibid.: 157). The message is that writing must be taken seriously, and if we don't come to writing with feelings, with our imagination, then it is not worth writing at all. This aspect is also emphasised by Stein (1931/1975: IX), who argues that, as writers, what we need to 'know is that there is no separation between thinking and feeling and the act of writing'. Stein explains that the capability of communicating and understanding what you do has to do with the other person's capability of doing the same work.

Issues around the multitude of power relations are central to a theory and method of situated writing. It draws on the contributions made by feminist and postcolonial scholarship, which problematised researchers' locations in relation to intersections such as gender, racialisation, class, heteronormativity, and beyond (hooks 1997; Dahl 2012; Scott 2018). Dahl (2012) illustrates the complexity of writing research when she invites her readers to accompany her on the road to writing, a space where (life) stories unfold, where a search for homecoming occurs, through a writing that emerges from the complexity of locations, through multiple languages in dialogue. From diverse sites of writing, critical explorations of power can be achieved, which in different ways expose the limits of criticism. Rendell (2010: 2) suggests that 'site-writing' includes engagement with the material, emotional, political, and conceptual practices of research, 'asking what is possible for an artist to say about a work, the site of the work and the critic herself and for the writing to still 'count' as criticism'. I argue that a situated writer learns about limits and writes to transgress them. Situated writing often exposes the limits of criticism, and at the same time, it can re-situate the work of an author to open up new interactive spaces. If we use writing with creativity and openness to shape knowledge, then it becomes a method of inquiry from which we find out things (Richardson 1994). To be able to reflect analytically upon the levels at work in situated writing as theory and method, I have created a set of questions and concerns in Table 1.1. It is inspired by Harding's (1987) definitions of epistemology, methodology, and method, and Richardson's (1994) criteria in 'Writing – a method of inquiry'. I suggest that this set of analytical questions is helpful in discussing the layers and complexities of situated writing.

Table 1.1 Translations of Situated Writing as Epistemology, Methodology, and Method

Epistemology is a theory of knowledge. Who can be a knower? What beliefs must pass in order to be legitimated knowledge? What kind of things can be known?	Situated writing is a theory of knowledge. Who can be a writer? Who is writing? What beliefs must pass in order for the writing to count as legitimated knowledge? What kind of things can be written?
A methodology is a theory and analysis of how research strategies can be shaped as applied practice. How does theory find its application in (and beyond) particular scientific disciplines and as interdisciplinary practice? How can we make use of interdisciplinarity to theorise?	Situated writing is a methodological tool, a theory and analysis of how research strategies can be shaped and applied. How does writing find its application in (and beyond) particular scientific disciplines and interdisciplinary practice? In what ways do the choice of topic and methodological design call for a particular form of writing? How does the writing shape interaction and dialogue with readers?
A method is a technique for creating and/or gathering material/evidence.	Situated writing is a method of inquiry, a practice by which you find out about yourself and the research topic. How is language put into use in writing? In what way is writing a creative activity?

A politics of location and translation: diffraktionsskrivande

This book is theoretically grounded in a politics of location and translation to promote situated writing, '*situerat skrivande*'. Inspired by making links between Haraway's (1988) politics of location, '*politisk lokalisering*', diffraction (see also Barad 2014), and Spivak's (1993) politics of translation, '*översättningspolitik*', I make use of feminist and postcolonial scholarship to promote diffractive writing, '*diffraktionsskrivande*'. Textual and visual compositions shape such writing through language, '*språk*', embodiment, '*kroppslighet*', power, '*makt*', and place, '*plats*', and promote ways of seeing, '*sätt att se*'. A politics of location contains a complex set of ideas and points of departure and has been the source of inspiration for scholars in feminist, gender, and intersectionality studies for decades. In this book on situated writing, the textual and the visual are intertwined in a politics of location. Situated writing, as it is developed in this book, extends the notion of sustainability to include writing as an embodied and living inquiry contextually tuned in to the geopolitics of institutions, inequalities, autobiographies, languages, and places (Livholts 2015c, 2017). It argues for slow writing to acknowledge unexpected situations, difficulties and failures, as well as creativity and euphoric moments in writing (cf. Bränström Öhman 2010; Ulmer 2017). The untimely academic novellas make use of a politics of location and translation by *sitting/seating* (in a professor's chair, a visiting chair, a sofa, on a concrete floor), *position/posture* (cultural and institutional embodied language, power, and knowledge), *spatial location and dis-location* (exclusion and inclusion socially and spatially), and *un/timeliness* (acting outside of the spaces where recognition and position are possible, spaces of misunderstanding and slow death). In untimely academic novella writing, the writer's narrativity is textually and visually tuned to see and feel specific situations in a process that involves thinking-writing-seeing-reading-feeling as a flow that moves from the furniture of the chair of solid materiality through white corridors and office spaces, to the snow angel with its dissolvable character set in a seasonal and historical landscape of three generations of women's lives (Livholts 2010a, 2010b, 2013).

One of Haraway's (1988) key points is the obligation to take responsibility for limiting our knowledge claims and not to speak from privileged positions in a generalising way (see also Mohanty 2003). Situated knowledge demands that the subject of the study is seen as an actor, an agent, and problematises the binary divisions of sex/gender, body/intellect, and so on. Knowledge is always situated and embodied, and it forms the foundations for the argument against unlocalised and irresponsible knowledge that does not account for the knower's position and ways of seeing. Haraway (1988: 583) talks about embodied vision and 'specific *ways* of seeing', asserting that there should be no invisible positions from which privileged subjects can speak. Thus, vision is used to create critical spaces that challenge dichotomies in language and research. Feminist objectivity is based on how visual systems work – technically, socially, and psychologically – and builds on situational and situated conversation. No subject or seeing position is non-problematic and whole, merely partial. As a narrative reflexive strategy, Haraway (2000: 102) argues that the metaphor of diffraction is useful to avoid a simplistic form for reflexivity that produces more of the same. She writes:

> I am interested in the way diffraction patterns record the history of interaction, interference, reinforcement, difference. In this sense "diffraction" is a narrative, graphic, psychological, spiritual and political technology for making consequential meanings.

Inspired by Haraway, Barad (2014) elaborates upon diffraction as a theory and method that is both optical and organic, and as such can be used in a multiplicity of ways. It does not cut the world into two, or separate us from them, this from that, but works through intra-action, difference within difference, and Barad (2014: 168) writes: 'cut together-apart (one move)'. Importantly, diffraction is a phenomenon that troubles dichotomies, rather than erasing them, and Barad (2014: 168) pays attention to the meaning of language:

> Diffract – dif-frange're – to break apart, in different directions (as in classical optics)
> Diffraction/intra-action – cutting together-apart (one move) in the (re)configuring of spacetimemattering; differencing/differing/diffe'rancing

Diffraction works in and through memories that Barad calls 'thick moments'. This way of understanding the moment is different from zooming in on a moment following a determined sequence of events (cf. memory work in Chapter 2). Instead, diffraction challenges narrative coherence and works through time and space in a dynamic way, characterised by the untimely.

> Diffractions are untimely. Time is out of joint; it is diffracted, broken apart in different directions, non-contemporaneous with itself. Each moment is an infinite multiplicity. "Now" is not an infinitesimal slice but an infinitely rich condensed node in a changing field diffracted across spacetime in its ongoing iterative repatterning.
>
> (Barad 2014: 169)

An interesting example of how diffraction can be used as a narrative strategy that invites the reader to translate, create, and re-create stories is Ehrnberger's (2017: 17) study, in which she makes use of diffraction as a research method to write multiple entangled stories through her design practice. 'I want to offer you my story for the creating of your story': *'Jag vill erbjuda dig min berättelse i skapandet av din berättelse'* [Swedish]. As her designer work materialises through the text, she enters into writing, and the reader is invited to enter too, to create their own stories. Another example of a narrative diffractive style is Holmquist (2019) textual and visual narrative method entitled The Production Novella. Through written memories from the design process and photographs from working sites, the novella method forms a language to communicate how globalisation changes the conditions for local industrial production.

Diffractive writing is also intimately intertwined with reading. Jones (2012, 2013) invites the reader to a multitude of time and space moments on a thinking journey Arendt. Moments of reading Arendt, and reading other's writing about Arendt, are interwoven with memories of traumatic events in the past. This becomes the departure for Jones as a writer to 'dive into' the story. She writes (Jones 2012: 58): 'Reading the book again like a writer, I began to understand what made its narrative so compelling: the storyteller had slipped into the story [...]'. Characteristic of Jones's writing is a diffractive style, composed through historical events, life scenes from the past and present, agency and resistance that seems to be untimely whenever they happen because they go against normative conceptions of what is a woman, what is love, what is possible.

My understanding is that diffraction has much to offer, both as a theory and as a method for situated writing. It re-conceptualises reflexivity by using an inventive approach that is both organic and optical, which can be used by researchers to situate and re-situate their selves, to shift writing positions, to see and see again, and to invite the reader to enter the story and engage in the creating of new knowledge. As Barad (2014) shows, diffraction works through the untimely and through memory. It rejects dichotomies and offers multiple ways of seeing, and its optical and organic characteristics are useful for theorising what can be done through life writing genres such as diaries and letters. In the context of this book, the untimely academic novellas' textual and visual shaping of snow and water offers diffraction patterns for the kind of 'narrative, graphic, psychological, spiritual and political technology' that Haraway (2000: 2) advocates. The snowflake is useful as a prism for narrativity. *Snow* is created through rainfall when water vapour is cooled to temperatures below zero degrees celsius. They take different shapes due to temperature and wind, from snow star to snowflake, and the movement of snow in the air when falling is aesthetically appealing. Snow is used in untimely academic novella writing to situate the writing body as a temporal imprint in rural space (Livholts 2010b). As the snow angel shifts through shades of whiteness and melts, it re-locates and re-situates the writer through water, entering into shades and layers and movements (Livholts 2013); as Ahmed (2017: 3) so beautifully writes: 'each movement making another possible, another ripple, outward, reaching'.

Feminist and postcolonial work around the world has shown how writing and language are embedded in complex relations of power, produced through layers of inequality and the geopolitics of situatedness (Anzaldúa 1987; Minh-ha 1989; Spivak 1993; Braidotti 1994; Faraneh 2014). Translation is an active practice that places language, words, expressions, and gestures in situations of understanding and communicating, where meaning is created through complex relations of power. In *Borderlands La Frontera: The New Mestiza*, Anzaldúa (1987: preface) writes from the embodied, physical, psychological, sexual, and spiritual borderlands of growing up as a 'border woman'. The shifts and complexities of living multiple identities 'is like trying to swim in a new element, an alien "element"', she writes. In her book, shifting languages interweave memories, time and place, to live, to keep images alive, to speak about abnormality, marginal spaces, fears, anger, images of flowers, of the wind. Changing and mixing languages from, to, and in between English, Castilian Spanish, North Mexican dialect, Tex-Mex, and Nahuatl, and all of these together create a new language of Borderlands. Another inspiration is Spivak (1993), who discusses the disciplining practices that are reinforced by English, which spurred me to read and reread some of the texts I think I know so well, and to practise the politics of translation, *översättningspolitik*.

On one occasion, I gave a lecture on feminist epistemologies, embodied and situated writing, for a class in which the students came from different cultural and national backgrounds and spoke diverse languages. I had prepared a short writing practice to promote reflection around writing, language, and power. The practice was inspired by a chapter I had written on situated writing in social work (Livholts 2017), in which I made use of the politics of translation developed by Spivak (1993). No one in the group had English as their mother tongue, and the instruction given to the students was to translate a short extract from Spivak's text in English into their mother tongue. This is the example I used, at first just showing the students the extract from Spivak's text, picking up on comments and thoughts and reflecting on and showing my own translation.

Spivak writes:

> Yet language is not everything. It is only a vital clue to where the self loses its boundaries. [...] The history of the language, the history of the author's moment, the language in-and-as-translation, must figure in the weaving as well.

> (Spivak 1993: 180 and 186)

I write:

> Ändå är språket inte allt. Det är bara en central ledtråd till den punkt där självet förlorar sina gränser. [...] Språkets historia, historien om författarens ögonblick, språket i-och-som-översättning, måste också få existera i de skapande processerna.
>
> (My translation from English to Swedish: Spivak 1993: 180 and 186. See also Livholts 2017: 98)

During the short session, there was silence in the room, and I perceived that intensive work was taking place among the students. Immediately afterwards, when I offered the opportunity for reflection to those who wished to share their experiences and thoughts after the session, I received diverse reactions. One reflection was that the short extract is so difficult in English that it is impossible to translate into Swedish, which was this student's mother tongue. Another was that the practice was useful and challenging because it unexpectedly evoked memories of situations in life, and particularly of situations in education around language use, both in English and in this student's mother tongue, which was Indian. A third response was put forward by a student who told me that they had several mother tongues, but had been forbidden to speak them as a child due to the particular country's politics towards the minority people who spoke them. This made the exercise particularly challenging, and the guidelines I had given excluded the possibility of working with several languages and/ or oppressed, forbidden languages. The translation practice that I had created presented this student with multiple dilemmas and a lack of time. I was asked to consider this complexity if I were to do this practice again.

Situated writing as theory and method is intertwined with the politics of both location and translation. Languages within local, national, and transnational contexts are diverse, and they include dialects and accents among the majority population, with the same national language spoken differently in the same region, as well as between regions and communities. Languages, both spoken and written, carry implications of evaluation, belonging, intimacy, and empowerment, and include or discriminate against and exclude minority and indigenous populations. At a certain point in my career, I thought that writing in English was liberating because it created a distance from the local and national context where I was located. Over the years, I have been re-thinking and re-evaluating this question.

Situated intersectionality: writing bodies/powers/spaces

> S/he who writes, writes. In uncertainty, in necessity. And does not ask whether she is given permission to do so or not. Yet in the context of today's market dependent societies, "to be a writer" can no longer mean to purely perform the act of writing. For a lay/woman to enter into the priesthood – the secret world of writers – she must fulfill a number of unwritten conditions. She must undergo a series of rituals, be baptized and ordained. She must *submit* her writing to the law laid down by the corporation of literary/literacy victims and be prepared to accept their verdict.
>
> (Minh-ha 1989: 8)

Situated writing is shaped through intersections of power relations, and it resists subordination to what Minh-ha, in the citation above, calls 'the corporation of literary/literacy victims'. As I have previously discussed, in my earlier work in particular (Livholts 2008, 2012a, 2015c), I wish to promote writing forms that de-hegemonise and intersectionalise writing by interweaving the *intersecting dimensions of power* that are present in both academic and personal life in a number of ways, including spatial location. The intention is to contribute to the critical study of intersecting relations of power by employing a shifting form of writing that challenges family and society to appear as embodied, emotional and loving, and at the same time scattered, dissolvable, and (re)formative (see also Livholts 2013: 189). The untimely academic novellas write bodies/powers/spaces through gender, whiteness, and class, situating the embodied self/selves in spaces, rooms, corridors, at tables and in relation to others. While gender contributes to subordination in a patriarchal hierarchical university, whiteness paves the way for privileges from which white bodies benefit, and the class dimension that I found to accompany my mother and grandmother through their lives negatively affected my life during my early years and as a young adult, at the same time as men in the same family led much more privileged lives (Livholts 2010b). My farming background brought a cultural dimension that seemed to distance my embodied self from intellectual legitimacy, and I perceived the change of space from rural farming space to urban university space as the loss of my writing body, which was situated in memories and landscapes. In this section, I reflect analytically upon the untimely academic novella as an example of making use of situated intersectionality, mainly taking inspiration from Yuval-Davis (2015).

Intersectionality studies constitute a vast field characterised by debates emerging from diverse viewpoints and methodological approaches. In this section, I interpret and translate Yuval-Davis' (2015: 5 and 6) main points of departure for situated intersectionality as a way of writing bodies/powers/spaces as part of situated writing:

> Situated intersectionality analysis, therefore, in all its facets, is highly sensitive to the geographical, social and temporal locations of the particular individual or collective social actors examined by it, contested, shifting and multiple as they usually are.
> [...] transcalarity – i.e. the ways different social divisions have often different meanings and power when we examine them in small scale households or neighborhoods, in particular cities, states, regions and globally; and of transtemporality – i.e. how these meanings and power change historically and even in different points in people's life cycle.

Yuval-Davis (2015) makes use of Haraway's critique that seeing from nowhere is ethically irresponsible and that there is a need to account for the social positioning of both researcher and researched. Thus, 'what we learn how to see' in terms of intersectionality requires us to continuously consider the dynamics and changeable situations and processes involved in diverse and interconnected lives. My argument is that it is challenging to find ways of employing such a practice without considering textual shaping. In the untimely academic novellas, the practice is to make use of both textual and visual practices through wording and photographs. Through diffraction, ways of seeing are grounded in a practice of scene-making and narration. When the camera sees, or the poetry is used as a sensory perception of seeing, it is made through analytical reflections about what it is the author sees. As one example, 'visualising, exploring, and disturbing whiteness' through the snow angel reconsiders privileges of whiteness, but also the oral histories that were told many times about my mother's childhood (Livholts 2010b: 121).

Situated intersectionality (Yuval-Davis 2015) makes use of critical race theory to include the positions of people who are both marginalised and privileged. Whiteness is often a 'silent' category that is reproduced predominantly by not being the focus of attention or identification. Frankenberg (1993) describes whiteness as a viewpoint from which a person sees other people, a position of structural privileges in life without having to identify this privilege. In line with Yuval-Davis (2015), she talks about the social geographies of racialisation, which include perceptions of diverse spaces and social relations in the city, neighbourhood, etc. In the exemplars of untimely academic novella writing, the racialisation process is part of a movement in between marginalisation and oppression as well as privilege. Whiteness is manifested in 'The Professor's Chair' (Livholts 2010a) partly through silence, over-voiced by gender and class, but also visualised through the colour of the white walls and psychological distress. In snow angel writing (Livholts 2010b), diverse forms of life writing and visual symbolism elaborate the power of whiteness. Diffractions of whiteness are problematised by photographing at different sites, in different landscapes and lights, during night and day and in the afternoon. As I show in this novella (Livholts 2010b: 104), whiteness has the transformable power of 'changing form and silently disappearing'. Several critical remarks can be raised against the snow angel novella. One aspect is the way in which it tends to also reproduce difference and evaluate darkness and/or light, and the power that whiteness gives me to re-invent privilege. Pease (2010) writes about the unmarked status of whiteness and the sense of entitlement that comes with privileges as a man, which he identifies as a cause for dominance and violence. There are examples of how I benefit from this unmarked status, for example, in a situation in which I illustrate a meeting with a group for equality and in a meeting room where I can see the names of academics who applied for promotion (Livholts 2013: 112):

> Among these names I saw my own and as I watched I felt how the reports on equality became a heavy burden on my legs. I realized how much work I had put into committees and boards and meetings all these years and I knew I could not go on in the same way anymore. I felt like a silent witness to the documented inequalities of this time, fostered by the statistics to know my place. On the other hand, an intriguing question is whether my previous name, Scheffer Kumpula, would have been among the names on that board? Livholts is an invented name. Did I invent privilege?

As I explain in my novellas, there have been several occasions when I have felt ridiculous and odd, in particular when doing the snow angel project. At the same time, I do think that the genres at play here, in particular the poetry and letters, allow for a critical examination of whiteness. As Warren and Kilgard (2001: 266) discuss, to visualise what is often silent is to set out to 'search for a language, a language of the body, to convey the complexity of this "character"'.

It is in the pluralities, and always contextual within the society in which we live, that gender is a process of becoming. In a theory and method for situated writing, processes of gendering are the result of becoming woman/women/I/She/Her/Eye in the context of doing work in the academy that is entangled with feminist theorising and living that life (cf. Ahmed 2017). Like whiteness, gender is constructed through diffractive writing. As a life writing project, the realities and relations of social life, the institutional and geographical, as well as relations of love, motherhood and living with sons, shape gender at different and intersecting levels. Connell's (2009) gender theory examines gendered relations of power from a global perspective and shows its multiple functions through the dynamics of structure and change in specific historical, cultural, and social contexts conditioned by colonisation, sexuality, and the relationship between the metropole and periphery. Direct power identifies gender inequality through statistics and representation, and highlights specific issues, like violence, and specific cases of inequality. Discursive power pays attention to how specific ways of talking are productive and contribute to both identity building and the disciplining of embodied practices. Postcolonial power interweaves the various geopolitical relations of ruling through a historical lens; for example, invasions, the re-organisation of gender relations, and how they are reproduced and/or changed today. Power relations are also shaped by the division of labour between spheres such as work and home and emotions that create positive and negative attachment, rejection and hostility, particularly in regard to sexuality, love, and parent-child relationships. This wider framework of gender is helpful for understanding gendered relations of power through their dynamics of difference within difference (cf. Barad 2014). The diffractive writing of gender in the untimely academic novellas involves letter writing to a woman friend, Maj, to be seated in a visiting chair, to live a life within the strict format of textual structures, to experience the mirroring of an ugly face, to feel depression breathing down one's neck, to be told that it will take a hundred years before an equal society exists, to feel the weight of the history of statistics, to cook, to care, to write, to dream, to struggle against unequal university structures that privilege men. As the Commentaries on 'The Professor's Chair' (Livholts 2010a) show (Halldorsdottir, Hyvärinen, Israel, Jackson, Misztal, Salter, Stanley and Tamboukou 2010: 169–172), the novella is a good example to spark discussions and critical reflections on the symbolism and realities of the main character's desire for the chair. I wish to thank the authors for their engagement in reading and commenting on this novella. Below, I have created a collection of short citations based on

'Commentaries on the Professor's Chair' in the issue of *Life Writing* where it was published in English:

> A position/a phallus symbol/discouraging/a tool rather than a site or posture/interdisciplinarity reads in-between-the-chairs/stealing it/I have stolen their language/becoming professor was not even a distant dream/I do not agree with the story's too pessimistic view/ it also has something to do with being creative/use of letters, verse, first-person, second-person/structures of power in academia/asks for more space for and in writing/a site to do things differently/is contempt for (at least some aspect of) academic life now almost obligatory?/I had somehow become 'chairable'/the heights were not so vertiginous after all/Perhaps the chair really needs more shaking!/the mystique of the Professor's Chair is the still-prevailing silence surrounding it/Let's all be chairless, surely?/

The analytical approach to intersectionality also includes class. Like whiteness and gender, I work with class as an interlocking and diffractive dimension of life writing. Brah and Phoenix (2004) write about how class is narrated in autobiographical studies alongside gender and racialisation. They address the question of class as 'entitlement/lack of entitlement' (2004: 78), discuss how class is lived and performed in different situations, and problematise how it interacts with whiteness. For example, markers of class can be related to situations of eating and food, as well as parenting, where gender, class, and colour shape the life circumstances of being a parent. They bring up how class, in the sense of a lack of resources and finances, creates embarrassment and how upward class mobility to middle classness compensates for women to help their children in school. By interviewing women, Sohl (2014) examined their upward class mobility in a Swedish context, looking at class in relation to gender, race, 'Swedishness', and sexuality. The study shows how doing well in education is seen to be crucial to their notion of mobility, moving out of the working class. Like other forms of power relations, class is geopolitically situated. In a Swedish context, Sohl (2014) highlights how (self-)evaluations of being good, capable and efficient, as well as racialised perceptions of Swedishness, are central to beliefs in upward mobility (cf. Scott 2018). In the untimely academic novellas, class is shaped and reshaped, lived and performed in the context of academic life, family relations, and society. Class differs, but is never totally separate, from gender and whiteness, and Sohl's (2014) inclusion of Swedishness in her analysis of class is contextually important to consider. In the untimely academic novellas, due to the problems

of academic legitimacy when writing differently, the mother/I moves
to different places in Sweden. These geographical movements, which
I perceive as forced because they are caused by the critiques of my different work, are linked with other movements across my family history.
This is visualised in the diverse names in the family, which extend beyond Swedishness to also signal connections to Finland and Germany.
The Professor's Chair (Livholts 2010a: 157) is a story in which the main
character expresses a desire for upward mobility in order to secure tenured employment and 'get rid of' her 'ugly face':

> P.S. I think about the title as a chair. At last I will have a long term
> employment after all these years. It will be good for me and the
> children. I might even get rid of my ugly face.

Other situations of lived experience in the novellas that demonstrate
the complexity of movements through class concern the changing relationships with the mother, stepfather, and sisters through education;
to become someone else in this case creates a movement from family
and rural space to university and urban space. In 'The Snow Angel and
Other Imprints' (Livholts 2010b), questions about seeking a home, and
unhomeliness, are central, questions that occur in the work of many
feminist scholars in different ways and national contexts (hooks 1999;
Farahani 2014; Ahmed 2017). Yuval-Davis (2015) emphasises the need
to work with sensitivity linked to geographical, social, and temporal
locations in order to promote situated intersectionality; however, she
does not show the path to this doing. As I have shown in my analytical
reflections on whiteness, gender, and class in the previous paragraphs,
the life writing genres are used as methods that allow for translocal
and trans-scalar understandings. Translocal means being aware of
how diverse categories of social division regain different meaning when
impacted by the different spaces within which they take shape. The
trans-scalar means that social dimensions of power take on different
meanings depending on whether they take place within a household,
a neighbourhood, a city, a region, or a state. In untimely academic
novella writing, the diversity of locations is intimately connected in
a multiplicity of ways, such as the landscapes of offices, corridors
and colours in academia shifting to the location, sounds and smells
through memories of rural spaces (Livholts 2010a: 160):

> Landscape of offices.
> Locked up.
> Colourlessness.
> Squareness.

She wobbled in her step. The walls moved. All of a sudden she was not walking down the straight and broad corridor, but a narrow winding path. She finds her room under the pressure of great strain, enters the door and touches the chest and the stomach in search for her breath. Someone has put on a bandage too tight around her chest. It is difficult to breathe.

Hunting hare and she is guard in the darkness and silence of the night.

Burning grass; she breathes spring and moves as fast as the whimsical wind.

The rhythmic movements of the horse running and the sound of clattering hoofs.

The smell of dust.
A fox screaming.

Note

1 I make use of a writing strategy of translation by infusing Swedish words into the text at specific moments. This is a way of allowing sensory perception and the sound of language and memories to be part of the writing. It places the context of language locally, nationally, and transnationally at the focus of attention.

2 Narrative life writing within and across mutable genres

Narrative is an emerging field of study within and across disciplines that takes diverse directions, philosophies, and analytical strategies (Andrews, Squire & Tamboukou 2009; Hyvärinen 2008; Stanley 2013; Witkin 2014; Livholts & Tamboukou 2015). In this book, the focus is on autobiography and life writing in narrative research, which have shown the historical and contemporary roles of writing lives in diverse historical, political, and social contexts (Stanley 1995, 2013; Jolly 2001, 2011; Plummer 2001, 2013; Livholts & Tamboukou 2015). As Jolly (2011: ix) states in *The Encyclopedia of Life Writing*, life writing is an umbrella term that 'encompasses the writing of one's own or another's life' and includes written forms such as diaries and letters and forms outside of the written such as artefacts, visual arts, photography, and film. This circumstance, that the 'documents of life' take different and multiple forms (Jolly & Stanley 2005; Lejeune 2009; Tamboukou 2015a), requires an openness to how they are shaped when put into practice by the writer/researcher in diverse projects, contexts, and disciplines, and how they develop as interdisciplinary practices. When discussing the tensions, disagreements, and exciting developments in life writing as a critical and creative practice, Jolly (2011: 878) contends that it is 'a mutable genre that can be at once critical practice, practice-based research and creative experiment'. This point of departure, that genres are transgressive and overlapping in their character, is central to this chapter's ambition to contribute to the development of situated writing as theory and method by making use of life writing genres such as memories, diaries, letters, poetry, and photography. As McNeill (2005: 7) suggests, life writing scholars who employ innovative writing methods need to understand genre as an analytical concept with unstable forms, focusing on 'what genres do, for whom and how?' The chapter begins with a section about the writing self that works as a platform for the diffractive multiple sites of the writer and takes inspiration from feminist literary fiction. Thereafter follow sections on each of the genres used in the untimely academic novellas, accompanied by short extracts as illustrations.

A single hand writes? The shaky character of the writing self

> [...] a single hand writes, but the self who inscribes, who is, is herself enmeshed with other lives which give hers the meaning it has. And it is not just "the author" who takes on an ontologically shaky character in these autobiographies, for so do "selves" in general.
>
> (Stanley 1995: 14)

How is it possible to see and see again through the life writings of the hand(s) that write(s)? Analytical questions about the writing self are challenging and thought-provoking, not least at a time when poststructuralist theories about the death of the author/subject coexist with the intensive activity of writing and image-making of our/selves in an increasingly digitalised society. Indeed, understandings of what the death of the subject means are the focus of many critical analytical discussions (Stanley 1995, 2015; Livholts 2015a; Tamboukou 2018). In her path-breaking work, *The Auto/Biographical I*, Stanley (1995) introduces a new theorising of the subject in feminist autobiography and beyond as a 'shaky character'. In this section, I take the illustrative formulation of subjectivity that is fleshed and gendered, intimately linked with social life and relations of power in a particular history and context, and shaped through textual and visual literacy, to promote a theory and practice of situated writing. As untimely academic novella writing in this book makes it possible to trace and re-think, the multiplicity of narrative life writing genres creates conditions for a writing that situates and re-situates embodied gendered selves in the contexts of intersectional relations of power, architectural institutional spaces, inter/disciplinary traditions and contexts. Thus, the writing selves transform through memories and stories, seasonally situated and reshaped through the storying of a woman's life, generations of women's lives, through motherhood(s), and through mirroring textual and visual appearances of the self.

Tamboukou (2018: 13) problematises the issues and tensions between poststructuralist approaches to the subject in feminist theory that promoted fragmentation and multiplicity, but did not take into consideration how 'the real', that is, materiality, entangled with discourses. Tamboukou suggests that narrative personae are useful as a theoretical approach for feminist narratology, which resonates well with the complexity of becoming a writing subject as an ongoing creative and reflexive process in the untimely academic novellas. These conceptual personae, as Tamboukou (2018: 4) argues, should not be mistaken for representatives of the author, but allow the author to work at a critical distance. 'It is a third person, the conceptual persona, not the philosopher, that says I, since there is always a multiplicity of enunciations and subjects in the work of philosophy'.

In the untimely academic novella, the hand that writes takes on the shaky character of a writing self who works at a distance. This is visualised through the language of naming. 'The Professor's Chair' (Livholts 2010a: 155) introduces the reader to a story about 'a woman's desire' to obtain a professor's chair. The embodied character of someone with *the name woman* is set within the architectural material and discursive space of a university, and the writing is enacted simultaneously by the author and the main character, a woman academic, in the novella and in other places. Thus, being not merely textual, the woman who writes, writes through and beyond the textual and fleshed self, extending to women in the plural, reshaped in relation to reflective surfaces, landscapes, textual expression, generations, socioeconomic class, mothering, and working life. The I/SHE/HER develops a subject of femininities, a gendering process of the self as 'woman', by which the untimely academic author conducts her writing through resistance. The narrative personae envision another future, a future self, passing through dead women, women in history. The writing I is always multiplied and, as Tamboukou (2018: 6) writes, has 'intervened in the social, political and cultural formations of her geographies and times'. For the purpose of illustrating the multiplicity of textual/ visual/selves at work in the novellas, I make use of Scriptio Continua below, a *writingwithoutspaces* (cf. Livholts 2015d; Küster 2016)[1]:

ISHEHerMeOneWomanANameIseeheratadistanceWritingI
TextualIMeCharacterISHEMotherISHEherMeOneIAWoman
AnameIseeheratadistanceMeCharacterImprintsofaSnowAngel
ISHEWaterMeIceSnowAngelMeltingISHEherMeOneIWomen
NamedMirroringSelvesonthefloooooooooooooorProfessorself
GrandmotherISHEWomanMirroringSelvesATemporalFigure
ArmsandLegsSpreadOutIamsorryMyFutureSelfWritingaSnow
AngelSHEUntimelyUglyyyyyFaceGuardingtheNightUntimely
WhitenessPrivilegedSelfIWorkingbodyDearDiaryDearMDear
UnnoticedDearFutureISHETragicSynicSelvesCreatureSelf
DepressionSelfSHEONEISeeingFurnitureSelfAngelSelfWaterSelf

SHEAuthorUntimelyAcademicNovellaWriterSelfISHECharacter
CreatureMeNotinAHundredYearsNotinAHundredYearsNotI
SHEWatchingHerataDistanceISHENamedWomanFrozenISelf
IceSelfWaterSelfIThefutureunseenfurnitureselfPassingthrough
bodiesSeeingHerthroughBluishCameraRealityWaterSelfDis
solvablebyTimeISHEHERONEWritingIWallpaperIWoman
MirroringSelvesATemporalFigureArmsandLegsSpreadOutthe
LanguageoffoldingclothHaditnotBeenUntimelySelfMotherSelf
WaterSe.

The unstable and decentred selves that emerge from the *writingwithoutspaces* illustrate the becoming of a gendered self, an invitation to
the reader to see fragments of the world from the perspective of the
writer. The untimely academic novellas raise questions and concerns
about the writing subject as someone with the name woman and, as
I developed in the previous chapter, this is a matter of intersectionality in terms of gender, class, and whiteness. I understand writing
as both discursive and material, a narrative process of wording and
re-wording, whereby the writing subject becomes author, researcher,
and writer as well as reader/audience. The shaky character of the
writing self is entangled with many other selves, histories, rooms and
houses, times, materials, and landscapes.

Feminist literary fiction: 'The Yellow Wallpaper' and 'Enter the Theatre'

It is in the spacious, friendly, and safe sabbatical writing space in the
self-catering accommodation in Lewes, near the 11th-century castle
during the spring of 2017, that I write the synopsis and first draft manuscript for this book. The window facing the garden is framed by red
roses, so one of the first things I do upon arrival is to place the table
and chair so that this window is my view each day while I write. As is
often the case, writing takes you along a pathway of memories of reading. I am reminded of citations I collected and was inspired by during
the early phase of this untimely academic novella writing. I search for
and find one by Virginia Woolf (1929: 41) from *A Room of My Own*:

> What were the conditions in which women lived, I asked myself;
> for fiction imaginative work that is, is not dropped like a pebble
> on the ground, as science may be; fiction is like a spider's web, at-
> tached ever so lightly perhaps, but still attached to life at all four
> corners.

To me, what Woolf wrote visualised is the relationship between writing fiction, the material realities of the writer, and the possibilities of using life writing to write about both everyday and academic lives. Woolf (1929: 4) further writes about the 'liberties and licenses of a novelist, to tell you a story' and that writing fiction in a particular context can 'contain more truth than fact'. Both these aspects are important and relevant for untimely academic novella writing, and I suggest that a theory and method for situated writing benefits from inspiration taken from fiction to create tone and voice, to reach out to readers, enabling them to see glimpses from the writer's perspective. As Moi (2008: 268) argues, 'A novel or a poem or a play, or a theoretical essay for that matter, is an attempt to make others see something that really matters to the writer'. In untimely academic novella writing, I use fiction to create imaginative scenes to elaborate upon the complexity of the untimely. This imaginative concept of time allows the envisioning of multiple layers of space and time as coexisting. The use of narrative life writing creates shifts in personae and the self, through memories of people, space, and place. In narrative research, there is a recognition that fiction is useful to write about the complexity of social life (Stanley 1995, 2013; Plummer 2001). As Plummer (2001) argued, the creating of life stories is an activity created and recreated by situating and re-situating themselves in different worlds. He contends that:

> One curious breed of life document, largely neglected by the social scientist, is the writing that takes on the form of a fictional novel but which is dealing with true events fully researched by the author.
>
> (Plummer 2001: 56)

There are good reasons to argue for the use of fiction as a way of dealing with true events in research and knowledge production, and the untimely academic novella constitutes one such example. Keen (2016: 9) proposes that life writing is a form of non-fiction with the 'capacity to invite feeling responses and to evoke readers' empathy'. Keen also brings up a question which I think is crucial; namely, that the tendency to place a clear-cut boundary between fiction and non-fiction is related to a presumption that non-fiction presents itself in a boring form and that the readers of fiction and non-fiction are two different categories (see also Richardson 1994; Stanley 1995). In line with these authors, I wish to emphasise that 'academic readers' are underestimated, and too often regarded as a homogeneous group of people. In fact, the diversity within and across communities of academic readers is vast.

Leavy (2013: 38) describes a number of goals for fiction as research practice. Fiction allows the researcher to portray lived experience in complex ways and to promote self-reflexivity, compassion, and engagement. Fiction potentially disrupts stereotyping processes and promotes social justice. There are several elements of using fiction in the untimely academic novellas. One aspect is related to how this particular writing emerged from attempts to write a novel. The first untimely academic novella – 'The Professor's Chair' – was published in Swedish in 2007 (Livholts 2007) and later in English (Livholts 2010a). However, by then, the draft of this text had existed for several years in the form of a crime novel. It was in 2006, while I was working with a feminist writing group (Bränström Öhman & Livholts 2007), that I coined the term 'untimely academic novella' for my work, and transformed my initial ambition to write a crime novel into the writing of an academic text (see also Kelly & Livholts 2014). An excerpt from 'The Professor's Chair' (Livholts 2010a: 159) illustrates how a fictionalised writing style is used as a method for situated writing.

Deported to the room of silence, cut off from the continuous conversation at the table, she becomes aware of the movable image in the window glass of herself and her colleagues. But they were not the only ones sitting there! Beside them, in a circle, a group of women sat on the cold concrete floor with their legs crossed. Text stripes were attached over their eyes and mouths. She was terrified when she saw them and wondered if it was the past or the future which presented itself in this way. Or, even more upsetting, death! She thought she had seen, if not dead, but rejected, silenced, expulsed women, and she asked herself if this would happen to her as well. Would she join the circle of ignored, ran down, invisible? If so, the next generation would be forced to pass through so many women's bodies and lives during all the hundred years to finally become professors.

To further describe how I was inspired by fiction to create a tone and style in the untimely academic novellas, I will now turn to the two feminist works of literary fiction that I selected as inspiration. These are the theorist, critic, and writer of fiction Hélène Cixous' (2004) essay 'Enter the Theatre' and the feminist author and theorist Charlotte Perkins Gilman's (1892/1989) novella 'The Yellow Wallpaper'.

Inspired by Cixous (2004), I make use of *untimeliness* as a strategy for narrating social change and the art of authoring. Cixous writes, among other things, about the untimely letter that is sent too soon or too late and refers to human relationships of understanding as not occurring at the same time. The becoming of authoring is a process that makes use of active listening as a strategy for forming characters of the past. Using this lag of misunderstanding, I elaborate with the 'cynic' and the 'tragic' as characters of agency in my novella (Livholts 2010a). Characters are created through the self as a shaky character (cf. Stanley 1995), by writing in the third person, which was initially inspired by the memory work method (Livholts 2015b), but then developed further as I was inspired by fiction and thinking and writing through characters. Untimeliness is an important theoretical location in feminist theorising. Grosz (2010: 48) argues that focusing on 'what is untimely, what is out of time' is helpful when re-exploring how bodies are situated in particular temporal and spatial sites. Barad (2014: 169) regards untimeliness as an important aspect of diffraction because it provides a method for us to understand time as 'broken apart in different directions', where each 'moment is an infinite multiplicity'.

My reading of Gilman's (1892/1989) novella is that patriarchal control and physiological distress are created by sceneries in which the colour of the wallpaper and the spatiality of a room are central. The woman in the text writes about her life and invites the reader into a 'house of illness' (Livholts 2015a). The emotions of the storyteller shift between reluctance to stay in the house and her obsession with the yellow wallpaper in her room, which she tears down to liberate the women who are trapped, creeping within the walls. I describe 'The Professor's Chair' (Livholts 2010a: 155) as 'a narrative about the act of writing, a story about creeping and sitting and searching for a posture and a place'. This struggle to be a thinking, writing subject in academia is intertwined with challenging the dominant social relations of gender. Gender is written through a diffractive lens. Gilman (1892/1989: 7) writes: 'There comes John's sister [...] I verily believe she thinks it is the writing which made me sick!' I develop my novellas using Gilman's writing strategy. I write about the problematic relations with other women and about participation in groups for equality. I also write about the changing emotions, fears, and fantasies that occur through the material spatiality of academic life and the sense of loss I feel in relation to the rural landscape where I grew up. Loss of orientation, tiredness, and whiteness represent this sensory space-making and a struggle with health. In this condition of societal and institutional constraints, I experience a sense of (self-)control, but also the emergence of multiple sites through which the shaky character of the writing I/Eye is created. As I write in the last untimely academic novella 'Writing Water' (Livholts 213: 181),

The writing and the text accompany me when I walk the streets of this small city, which I often do. I feel that my life is shaped by the existence of the novella, as if I am both that woman in the text striving for the chair and at the same time watching this story.

Memory work: writing in mo(ve)ments

I walk across the university building, grey stone and wooden floors, moving from one space to another separated by heavy glass doors, using the palm of my hand and the weight of my body to push them open. It is late autumn 2001 and I am on my way to the library to register my dissertation. I wear a long blue skirt, a dark red jumper and black shoes with laces, and I feel the weight of the dissertation that recently came from the press, in my bag. I have chosen bright colours for the cover, lilac and pink. As I hand over the dissertation to the librarian, she flips through it and looks surprised. She tells me that this dissertation can't be properly categorised within the format for how a dissertation is supposed to be written, with an introductory framework and a section for peer-reviewed articles. My dissertation has a third and even a fourth part and several possible endings. Part III is "The thinkingwriting subject: an individual work of memory", and Part IV "Untimeliness and social change" outlines three different endings, including a theatre, and an untimely letter.

(Memory written 28-06-2018; rewritten 02-08-2018)

Working with memories is a design element in the untimely academic novella that was inspired by the memory work method developed by Haug et al. (1987) and the film and photography by Kuhn (1995, 2010), and I have later been inspired by forms of the method conceptualised as collective biography (e.g. Davies & Gannon 2006; Wyatt et al. 2011). In this section, I present the main analytical basis of memory work as theory and method.[2]

The origins of memory work go back to the 1970s and the second wave of the women's movement for emancipation to promote subjugated voices and silenced stories to be heard and become public. The philosophical and theoretical points of departure of memory work are intimately linked with a politics of location and translation and to an understanding of the self as narrative personae that situates and re-situates the writer through multiple sites of remembering. Memory work relies on several *philosophical and theoretical* underpinnings. It emerges from the poststructuralist critique of structuralism, arguing against grand narratives, a linear view of time and the division of subject and object.

Memory work aims to bridge the divide between theory and practice and the intersections between personal experiences, societal structures, and multiple relations of power, to allow the category of women as agents and their life conditions to be seen in a multiplicity of contexts. One of the core issues for memories is meaning-making through language and discourse, which promotes memory workers to engage in writing and seeing in order to develop critical awareness and analytical reflexivity towards the limitations of wording life experiences. However, memory work is also based in materialist feminist epistemologies, grounding abstract notions of language in concrete situations in life and situations where inequalities are reproduced. As Hyle et al. (2008: 7) point out, memory work potentially gets at things we tend not to remember because they are not valued and are suppressed by discursive practices of forgetting linked with class, ethnicity, gender, physical limitations, experiences of exclusion, and marginality. Working with memories potentially brings about an alternative discourse, allowing us to see things differently by grounding language in materialist practices.

I often make use of words such as fragments, moments, snapshots, images, scenes, and clues to illustrate how I understand memories as textual and/or visual imprints in the context of narrative life writing. An analytical concept that I think is helpful to better understand the width of memories in writing and as visual symbolism is the conceptualisation of them as *'archaeological artefacts'* (Hyle et al. 2008: 7). As Haug et al. (1987: 47–48) write, 'Stepping back into the past, we embark upon a form of archaeology' where we 'discover fragments of an architecture that we then begin to reconstruct'. Plummer (2001: 232–54) problematises how memories create meaning at different, interacting levels. Personal memory is related to psychological processes of remembering that include what and how a particular person recalls and does not recall. Narrative memory is shaped by our motivations to select particular stories, which create our experiences and memories. In their complexity, memories contribute to 'shaping how we feel, how we listen, how we touch, how we smell, how we breathe and live in the world' (Plummer 2013: 215). In memory work, time has a transformative force by making it possible for the past, present, and future to coexist, but the 'narrative mode of interlinked stories' is not coherent (Haug et al. 1987: 52). In their study on memory and emotion, Crawford et al. (1992: 51) addressed the issue of truth and memory:

> The memories are true memories, that is, they are memories and not inventions or fantasies. Whether the memories accurately represent

past events or not, however, is irrelevant; the process of construction of the meanings of those events is the focus of memory work.

Writing is at the heart of memory work as a method; it makes possible the creation of textual memories and is also a technology for interpreting images. An important aspect is that although the moment is in focus, the process of doing memory work means working with technologies of writing, speaking, reading, listening, and seeing, which create *mo(ve)ments* (Davies & Gannon 2006: 7; Livholts 2015b). Writing about concrete situations allows us to note fragments and scenes from the flow of events in everyday life. The creative writing process allows the transgression of boundaries between academic, literary, and everyday communication, and the recommended technique of writing in the third person creates distanced seeing in relation to situations in the past, and sensory perceptions and emotions when working with memories (see also Haug 2008). Among scholarship that uses these writing methodologies in memory work today, there is diversity in the practices of using the third or first person. Indeed, methods are continuously being reshaped when put into use in diverse research and pedagogical contexts. Haug and her co-workers (1987) raised issues around the body, gendered relations of power, and knowledge production. This connectivity of the relationship between single memories and consequences such as restrictions of bodily movement, disciplining of the self in different situations across personal and public lives shows the material consequences of discursive practices. Kuhn (1995), who worked with textual and visual materials, shows how photographs and film can be used as triggers for memory work, and how textual and visual methodologies are intertwined and contextualised by family relations and nation. Examples of memory work studies include space, communication and telephony (Bryant & Livholts 2007; Livholts & Bryant 2013), emotion (Crawford et al. 1992), education (Widerberg 2016), fatherhood and family (Pease 2008; Widerberg 2010), ageing men and social change (Barber et al. 2016), intersectionality studies (Berg, 2008), and rural studies (Bryant & Livholts 2014). The renaming of the memory work method as collective biography (Davies & Gannon 2006: 3) marks changes in applied practices of 'technologies of telling, listening and writing' and emphasises poststructuralist theory when working with memories as mo(ve)ments in the creation of discursive meanings and selves. The example from collective biography used by Wyatt et al. (2011) is based on email correspondence and the participants' reading of Deleuze. This collective process takes the form of letter-writing across space and time and the becoming of interlinked subjectivity and the creating and re-creating of rooms and spaces.

As I have argued in my previous writings on the memory work method (Livholts 2015c: 168–171), working with photographic images extends analytical creativity and reflexivity, and contributes to situated writing as theory and method (see also the section on poetry and photography). A photograph freezes the moment, and because it portrays environments, with or without people, it is infused with a certain power of speaking the truth (Riessman 2008). Thus, technologies of writing, telling, and listening in memory work are enriched by technologies of seeing. Sontag (2007: 87) describes photographs as pieces in an ongoing history, noting that 'one photograph, unlike a painting, implies there will be others'. Again, the power/knowledge relationship, which permeates discourse and narrative in their interrelation, reminds us that looking is not an innocent activity, but 'operates as the foundation of a system of classification and control' (Kuhn & McAllister 2006: 4). In a similar way as texts depend on intertextual connections, when working with images it is important to think about how the *mo(ve)ment* is interlinked with the occurrence of other images and their discursive and narrative structure. One of the notable scholars who worked with images through photography and film scenes in memory work is Kuhn (1995, 2010). The main question for Kuhn was the way in which images, such as photographs or film scenes, could constitute *pretexts* for memories. Kuhn presents photographs as 'triggers' that evoke specific memories due to their role in a complex pattern of social relations, cultural contexts, and historical moments. Bringing in the spectator's agency and interpretative acts in relation to an image, Kuhn conceptualises a technology of looking from the intertext of discourses: 'memories evoked by a photo do not simply spring out of the image itself, but are generated in a network, an inter-text of discourses that shift between past and present, spectator and image, and between all these and cultural context, historical moments' (Kuhn 1995: 14).

Memory work is a method that I first used in my PhD dissertation (Livholts 2001/2011), whereby memories from the main topics of the articles in the dissertation constituted themes enabling me to work with situations that I found important to help me situate and re-situate, think and re-think the production of knowledge. I regard the memories in the untimely academic novellas as architectural artefacts that connect time and space through the linking of memories from diverse situations in my working and personal lives during the process of producing knowledge. The timeline is interrupted by early memories of childhood, the rural spaces, and academic spaces and university buildings. The styles and genres in which I write memories in the un-timely academic novellas shift and are contextually shaped by the agency of doing through dreaming, scenes from water-skiing as a child, the material of water. They are often written in a poetic style, and I think it is particularly illustrative of memory work that the separation between words and images is blurred. Rather, memories are scenes and fragments by which the world is seen and they constitute how we come to know it. In this sense, memories in untimely academic novella writing are grounded in the philosophies of becoming of a shaky character of a self who is situated and re-situated throughout the writing.

Diarist and epistolary forms: sculpting lives

In this section, I reflect analytically on the contributions of diaries and letters in promoting situated writing as theory and method from the example of the untimely academic novella. I begin with an extract from the (research) diary I kept during the late spring and early sum-mer of 2017, while I was staying in the small town of Lewes near the University of Sussex in England.

Lewes 12th May 2017

I was up early this morning (again!), and felt already when I woke up that some of the things that troubled me yesterday were clearer, although still problematic. I looked at the list of things I must remember to take into consideration when writing my book, and it is obvious to me now that, although there are many challenges, ethical concerns have increasingly appeared as the greatest obstacle. Ever since I wrote The Snow Angel, *I have felt that the power of narrative is very strong, that publishing letters and diaries that include family members is sensitive and occurs differently when I read them now several years later: also that I myself have become part of the story world that I created. I want to end this project and get out! I have sent my book synopsis to a publisher and am waiting for a reply. In the meantime, I keep on writing with readers in mind, but from the experience that readers of my work have come from unexpected fields such as art and design, it is difficult to imagine what the readership for this book will be. Perhaps I should just try the (forbidden) strategy of not thinking at all that I know my readers, or even if there will be any. (Which I surely can't write in a book I want a publisher to publish!) The other day, I read something interesting in the afterword to* The Yellow Wallpaper, *a book that inspired my own writing so much. It was written by Elaine R. Hedges and reveals the information that it was not easy for Charlotte Per-kins Gilman to get her story published. It had been passed on to someone called Horace Shudder, editor of* The Atlantic Monthly, *a prestigious magazine in America at that time. He rejected Gilman's novella with a short note saying: 'Dear Madam, Mr Howells has handed me this story. I could not forgive myself if I made others as miserable as I have made myself!'[3] I dwelled on these words, and couldn't help it that they somehow amused me, thinking that unfortunately a publisher could say a similar thing about my work. I can feel that myself when I read it, and imagine how miserable it must make readers to see the inequalities of our time!*

* * * *

Diaries and letters are historically established and blurred genres for auto/biography and life writing, continuously emerging among the diversity of writing and communication that can be found in archives and that we see in digitalised societies (Stanley 2015; Tamboukou 2015a; Kruster 2016; Stanley & Jolly 2017). This diversity, as well as the perceptions that we tend to develop through our relationship to diaries and letters, opens up space for questions and concerns about their character and form, the relationship between lived and narrated lives, and how the digitalisation of letter-writing poses questions about the 'death of the letter' (Jolly & Stanley 2005; Stanley 2015). Stanley (2004: 201) addresses this condition through a set of questions that illustrate the complexity of the ways in which diary and letter-writing are transforming:

> Why don't I (do I?) write letters? I do write "a diary, of a kind"; and, while I used to worry about not keeping "a proper diary", this has evolved into something I'm comfortable with, fieldwork notebooks that I write rigorously at important research junctures. However, perhaps emails serve the same purpose for me that letters used to? Or is it that my letters were never very important, being "mainly business", or that I am, oh horror, locked into "personal" writings rather than interpersonal ones? But then, what about my public writing, the articles and book chapters and books that I produce for publication purposes, and always with an audience in mind?

As an untimely academic novella writer, I am a (periodic) diary and letter writer who makes use of these blurred genres to document and communicate events and situations from my academic and personal lives. I view my writing as interlinked fragments that emerge over time and as 'stories that respond to the world, rather than represent it' (Tamboukou 2015a: 156). Furthermore, I understand the narrative power that this writing creates over time to extend both before and after the writing, transgressing the text to living a life, what Herman (2002) calls a 'story-world'. I am both writer and reader in this situated writing project and become emotionally involved in the context of the storyworlds I create in dialogue with my imagined readers. As Herman (2002) illustrates, in storyworlds, narrative representation is linked with emerging consciousness and emotion to impact upon and reveal what it is like to live through this storyworld. All forms of representation are situated and interpreted within a specific discursive context or occasion for telling. This means considering that the researcher/interpreter is re-constructing a story by making use of the storyworld, including the textual medium and the plot and characters. This narrative interpretation is communicatively situated. Both forms of writing are responding to real-life experiences, situations, relations, and thoughts, but the way in which I shift and change between and within them to perform encounters, relations, situations, spaces, thoughts, and dreams shapes them in specific ways. As I explained in the section on literary fiction and the theatre, I am inspired by the creating of characters, plots and relations, as well as notions of space and colour, from Cixous' (2004) theatrical writing and Perkins Gilman's (1892/2012) literary fiction of yellow wallpaper. While letters are used more frequently in 'The Professor's Chair' (Livholts 2010a) and 'The Snow Angel and Other Imprints' (Livholts 2010b), the diary appears more in 'Writing Water' (Livholts 2013).

* * * *

Lejeune (2009: 173) has theorised the diary as an open and formative document that 'sculpts life as it happens and takes up the challenge of time', and suggests (2009: 194–196) that diary writing has four functions: (1) The first is to express oneself, which allows one to release emotions and thoughts, and to communicate. Making use of writing is an act of expression and separation that connects the body (hands, fingers) with the pen, or the keyboard, into a form of meaning-making through words. This may include the destroying of your diary to allow for new writing. The well-known beginning, 'Dear Diary', is an act of communication towards the paper, the machine, and/or the self that may end if there is an act of communication in real life. (2) The second function is to *reflect*, which potentially has an analytical and deliberative effect. The diary allows the writer to develop thoughts and reflections, make notes on the everyday, and/or write about crises and difficulties. The writer is also a reader of the diary, and in this way creates a distancing from the self. (3) The third function is to *freeze time*, and Lejeune (2009: 195) writes that this function means to 'build a memory out of paper, to create archives out of lived experience, accumulate traces, prevent forgetting [...]'. Diary writing bears a complex relationship to time and memory. For the diary writer, the writing occurs in the present, documenting memories from the past and can be a powerful tool for memory against forgetfulness. (4) The fourth function (Lejeune 2009: 195) is to take *pleasure* in writing through 'a flow of energy that courses through the practice of writing'. Here, it is important to consider the situatedness of the writing body, and what I have suggested is a performance of many selves in space and time. As Tamboukou (2015a) writes, the diary is not separated from the body, but is constituted as a living body.

I find the expression 'sculpting life' to be a good way of creatively expressing diary writing as a form of art-based aesthetic practice aiding creativity and analytical reflexivity. It points to the creative interconnectivity between embodied life and textual shaping that I demonstrate in my untimely academic novellas. However, in my case, they have a double effect. They sculpt life through documentation and reflection, and as a communicative act they attempt to reach out to readers. However, they also sculpt life as a space of constraints, tiredness, and failing health, and at the same time the writing is health promoting. Over time, I have felt that the diary has become, in part, my parallel life – 'that my life is shaped by the existence of the novella' (Livholts 2013: 181). Thus, a question actualised through my own diary writing is how the diary has shaped my life over time and how *not writing* a diary does not mean that I stopped writing. I still experience that the not-writing of a diary is a companion, a notebook for writing that offers a writing space from the body, a complex shaky character of a self who narrates my academic and personal lives as intimately entangled. Lejeune (2009) admits to belonging to those few loose-page writers and not the notebook writers, which for me was a relief to read, because my perception was that a real diary should always be written in a notebook. I used to keep loose pages in different places in my room when I was young, and my diary for the untimely academic novella has been written periodically, mostly on the computer and to some extent as isolated documents, both on paper and in the computer. I lost one of my longest periods of diary writing when my computer crashed, and I have also deliberately deleted/destroyed longer periods of writing. This experience resonates with Tamboukou's (2015a: 151) problematisation of the material infrastructure of diaries. She writes that the diary

> [...] is therefore not simply a collection of memories or thoughts, a text or an image but a living body, an assemblage of space/time/

matter components that keep making connections with the body of the diaries as well as that of its multiple readers.

* * * *

'Dear Maj, I hope you endure my letters. At times I am afraid you will get too tired of listening to the endless problems academe has brought to our lives'. This is how the first letter in 'The Professor's Chair' begins, addressed to a friend, voicing troubled thoughts from academic life (Livholts 2010a: 156). Jolly and Stanley (2005) discuss how letters are shaped by situational contexts that are more social than individual and suggest that it is possible to identify a particular epistolarium in the analysis of letters through the distinctive way in which one writer's letters are different from those of other authors.

Stanley (2004) has shown the rich contribution made by letters to social research and has developed a theory and analysis of epistolary narrative based on three dimensions: (1) Letters are *dialogical* and as such a communicative act of correspondence, which means that how we understand dialogue theoretically and shape it when writing letters is central. (2) Letters are *perspectival*, written in the moment, and connecting with other moments. Writers make use of voice and tone and personae to develop humour or strictness. (3) Letters are *emergent*, which means they do not fit into a specific form or content structure, but are developed through the ethics that letter writers utilise over time. In the writing of letters in the untimely academic novella, the relationship between the letter writer (me, Mona) and the receiver (my friend Maj) builds on an existing friendship and thus confirms that referential and 'real-world' connection (Jolly & Stanley 2005: 95). However, as part of the project of writing untimely academic novellas, the letters are never sent. Nevertheless, they reflect ongoing conversations and reflections about academic life. The perspective is that of the letter writer, and as publicly published letters, they can be read by anyone. Tamboukou (2015a: 155) discusses how the narrative mode of letters is characterised by openness against closure and coherence, and 'provide[s] multiple perspectives on the same event'.

Poetry and photography: creating word-images and self-portraits

Sometimes at a research seminar birdsong can be heard
We drink coffee and eat blueberry cake
It is like a poem, the scrape of the plastic spoons

A sort of cheerfulness like poetry in its ability to dream
It is so lovely to be able to dream
To dream together in a seminar
It is poetry that is read
in the rain alone on a platform
as the trains come and go
The heavy clock of opportunity
That everything exists and can exist
It is right after the rain
The grass heavy
and the gravel
The clock cuts through time with its knives
We can recall without thinking
We talk to begin thinking together
You get to write what you want
You can write however you want
It does not matter as long as we live

The poem by Hallgren (2015: 87) that introduces this section makes use of sensory perceptions such as smell and colours, weather and movement, and the agency of reading, thinking, talking, and writing in a seminar room. I read this poem as an invitation to a seminar room which coexists with rain, trains, travelling, different times and spaces, remembering, imagining, dreaming, and writing. Hallgren (2006, 2015, 2017) makes use of writing as a method in the context of situated knowledge, poetry, and literary composition. In Hallgren's work (2015: 109), poetry, fiction writing, and feminist philosophy inspire knowledge production by making use of writing as a method.

In this section, I analytically reflect on how *(academic) poetic writing and photographic acts contribute to theory and method for situated writing* characterised by the pace of *slowness*. I emphasise how poetic writing as a method is intimately intertwined with image-making, both in the sense of seeing through words and in combination with visual symbols and artefacts captured through photography, such as a chair, an angel, and water. I consider how they actively *shape spaces* by including glimpses from the writer's rooms, sites, and viewpoints and the creative and emotional forces for situated writing of the subject/self.

Throughout the process of rereading the novellas for the purpose of writing this book, I was struck by how the poetry aesthetically opens up opportunities for many possible readings and interpretations. Looking back on the shifting forms of textual and visual representations and the intention of creating a critical, creative, and reflexive space, the poetic language that shapes the professor's chair, the snow angel, and writing water invites the reader to scenes where bodies, furniture, buildings, and landscape, along with past, present, and future, are entangled. The desirable gaze, seeing the furniture, caressing along the cloth of the red chair. The protagonist with the name 'woman' makes angels in the snow, leaving an imprint that erodes with time.

The poetics of writing angels in the snow is shaped in a diversity of weather conditions, in wet snow, soft snow, in different times and places (Livholts 2010b: 104):

> She is lying on the frozen ground, embraced by soft, dry, powdery snow.
> Face touches sky.
> Arms and legs spread out.
> The language of folding cloth marks a temporal figure.
> Carefully rise to upstanding position,
> Hold balance and step out of the imprint,
> Watch the contours of a Snow Angel.
> Snow beneath her jacket; a miniature stream of water is running down her neck. Changing form and silently disappearing.

My first encounter with poetry as a theory and method of inquiry was when I read Audre Lorde's (1984) *Sister Outsider.* I perceived Lorde's poetry as a form of passionate writing from the body, and this writing made it possible to understand the multiplicity of intersecting power relations in society (see also Lorde 1997). Lorde (1984: 37) states that 'poetry is not a luxury', but intimately connected with the possibility of building hopes and dreams through language and from language to ideas and to action. 'Poetry is the way we help to give name to the nameless so it can be thought', she writes (1984: 37). Relating to the questions I formulated in Figure 1.1 (p. 94, below), poetic writing addresses important aspects of the writers' craft such as writing silences, and actualises questions such as 'Who can write?' 'Who is writing?' 'What can be written?' and, in addition, 'What can be thought?'

Poetic inquiry in research and education is a growing field in qualitative studies (Gunaratnam 2011; Eng 2012; Leavy 2013; McCullis 2013). McCullis (2013: 88) provides insight into a diversity of ways in which poetry can be used as a tool to view and write data, one that is helpful in employing empathic and creative perspectives. Theoretically, *language* becomes a transformative space through poetic writing and creates what Leavy (2015: 97) calls '*a third space*', '*a third voice*', to mediate experiences that cannot be expressed through other forms of language. I believe that this question of creating a third space through writing is important, and as Gordon (2015) shows in her study of creative life writing, dialogical spaces for writing can also promote personal freedom. McCullis (2013: 89) suggests that the set of analytical questions posed by Stein (1931/1975) are helpful: 'What do the poems feel like? What do they mean? Toward whom and what do the poems point? Who and what are the poems about?'

In a three-hour walking project, Rendell (2001: n.p.) makes use of angels as a mode of writing as narrative practice, a way of thinking and exploring spatial practices differently. Rendell suggests diverse ways of analytical thinking for wapping/walking angels. The first is a thinking space through angels, and Rendell asks readers to consider the ways in which exchanges take place in banks, libraries, or post offices, such as words, items, and letters, and the agents of exchange, such as guards and vehicles. Another dimension is the social, which proposes analytical reflexivity in regard to how angels represent relations between people, objects, and places. In theoretical terms, the figuration of the angel promotes an *emancipatory practice of 'between-ness'*, where the angel is (Rendell 2001: n.p.) 'an emancipatory impulse, allowing movement "between" places, times, people, things and ideas' that 'allows ways of imagining new spatialities, temporalities and socialities'. In the untimely academic novella (Livholts 2010b), I show how angel writing can be shaped as a theory and method of critical interrogation when mapping embodiment and spaces of whiteness as privilege. Poetry and photographic acts play a significant role in visualising and conceptualising what would often otherwise remain unarticulated as a silent discourse for the privileged subjects who benefit from it. As I have written in the commentary to 'The Snow Angel and other Imprints' (Livholts 2010b: 121–122), 'visualizing a form of embodied whiteness alters my view of the landscape'. Poetic writing and photographic acts of making snow angels invite both their creator and the readers to 'watch its becoming and reflect on the meaning of contemporary imprint in a place called both rural and northern'.

There is an intimate connection and tension between poetic writing and the narrative approaches of wording/writing. As Berger (1984/2005: 21) writes, poetically about poems, they recognise that 'what has been experienced cannot disappear as if it had never been'. Time plays a pervasive role both as theory and as method in the untimely academic novellas, in which poetic language is used to create place beyond a specific notion of time. Time is also a forceful actor that speaks the language of power; time invites the cynical and the tragic; friendship, love, waiting, tiredness, failing health, and a letter that arrives after the recipient has moved (Livholts, 2013: 178):

Had it not been too late, I would have claimed I am writing
water,
In the age of untimeliness.
The letter is sent too soon, too late.
The recipient has moved.

* * *

Written in the layers of ice, cracks, breaking the line,
Had it not been too late,
I would have claimed that I am writing water.

* * *

Through all uncountable years of metaphoric captivity I was
always writing water;
but it was just now when you were leaving with the train and the
lake threw rain on our faces,
that I was astonished to know this.

In untimely academic novella writing, textual and visual auto/biographies are employed as a narrative strategy, and there is an intimate relationship between poetry and photo-wording. Initially, the use of photographs as 'triggers' for the writing of scenes lent inspiration drawn from the memory work method (Kuhn 1995: 2010), but I have continued to develop this writing as a situated theory and practice for ways of seeing (Berger 1972; Haraway 1988). Engaging with the theory and practice of the situated writer at work, I have increasingly come to regard it as a form of self-portrait with a performative and life-shaping role, whereby geographical space and nature are part of the writing body. The title 'The Professor's Chair' came early to my mind during the writing of the first novella, followed by 'The Snow Angel' and 'Writing Water'. It was the metaphorical and performative power of these words as interpretations and sensory perceptions of objects, landscapes, and (inter-)disciplinary practices in academia that created movements in the writing. Drawing on my untimely academic novellas as examples, I wish to theorise the making of word-pictures. As Stanley (1995: 25) writes,

> [...] photographic and other literal or memetic visual images are not the only sources of 'pictures'. Others can be built up in words themselves [...]. These word-pictures can be and often are much more powerfully present in the mind's eye than the literal images provided by photographs and film.

One of the functions of visual symbolism in the untimely academic novellas is as an 'interruptive agent' (Livholts 2010a: 121). Kuhn and Emiko McAllister (2006) argue that although photographs are still acts, they have the capacity to interrupt present time by reminding the viewer of another time, a specific situation. The power of the maker, the photographer, when creating an image, is central, and so the theoretical understanding of what is an image to the researcher and the practice of photographing in research should always be discussed. When using words and images as textual/visual representations in research, the researcher needs to consider how specific information about a photo alters its meaning. In the example of the snow angel, this concerns translations of privilege, but also nuances of whiteness and emotions and discomfort of reflexivity. By engaging in critical reflection on how light and dark are evaluated by me as a photographer, how landscape scenes are described in the photo-making and how the embodied imprint shifts between bluish and greyish, it is possible to transform whiteness through the light of the landscape. Inspired by Manning, Ulmer (2018) makes use of photo-poetry in a work called 'minor gestures', where photographic acts are entangled with poetic writing in the context of everyday spaces and movements. Photography is used to document the visual experiences in the local community that provoked and remained with the author. Ulmer (2018: 321) asks questions such as 'What is research?' and 'How can it be written and where does it happen?' '[M]inor gestures encourage us to slow down, wake up, read more, and listen and respond to everyday environments'.

In *Ways of Seeing*, Berger (1972: 10) states that 'Every image embodies a way of seeing' and also that seeing and situating are intimately intertwined. Thus, seeing a landscape means at the same time to be situated within that landscape; seeing an artwork from the past situates us in history. However, the ability of the situating self to claim ways of seeing in historical context depends on their privileges to be able to situate or not situate themselves in history. Berger and Mohr (1982/2016) have created a theory and method, a practice for photography, which has inspired me to further develop analytical reflections for situated writing as theory and method: 'What did I see?' write Berger and Mohr (1982/2016: 43), and explain how a photographer wants to know how the photographs are read and interpreted, or perhaps even rejected by the spectator. Also, they stress that the photographer wishes to tell the story of the photograph and that a photo itself is rarely perceived as sufficient. Berger and Mohr (1982/2016: 40–41) argue that to become a photographer, it is important to take self-portraits in order to understand 'the embarrassment, the worry, even the panic that people may experience when being photographed'. It has been an unexpected experience to learn that as the years pass, I perceive an increasing vulnerability when talking and writing about my untimely academic novellas. I further develop this aspect in the last section on vulnerable writing and relational ethics. At times, I have experienced embarrassment, worry, and even panic. The power of narrative life writing, the diffractions that are possible to write as moments, the elaborating with textual shaping, the letting go of conventions, and taking risks are all representations of the shaky, diffracted self, and of the continuous force of writing, even when I am not writing.

Together, the poetic writing and photographic acts in the untimely academic novellas are parts of a textual visual *self-portraiture* in a theory and method of situated writing. The mirroring of the self and the many imprints of the writing body form a narrative encounter that occurs as diffractive in a variety of places and spaces in the novellas. It involves the imagination of a self within the white walls of university corridors, a self that is textually and visually narrated through the lens of the camera by the photo of a university building, of snow angels, and water. Theoretically, Tamboukou (2015b: 78) argues that an analytical strategy for the study of the self-portrait 'calls for close attention to the historical, social and cultural contexts that condition the emergence of the work of art under consideration'. Following from this insight, the question of re-contextualisation needs to be considered, as part of which, making a work public is an important question. What happens when the context of the artwork changes? This, in turn, generates complexity and challenges the methods for doing self-portraiture by making use of words and image-making. It is also a question about what can be written from the viewpoint of ethics for self and others: who is included in the self-portrait when doing life writing? In the next section, I conclude with some analytical reflections on relational ethics and vulnerable writing.

The sustainability of situated writing: equality, vulnerability, and the ethics of change

'What then made writing this kind of thesis possible? My first and unequivocal answer would be – other feminist texts' (Livholts 2001/2011: 2).

As a PhD student in social work during the late 1990s and the beginning of the 2000s, feminist and postcolonial scholarship gave me 'permission' to work with textual shaping as a methodological strategy (Livholts 2016a). In the introduction to my dissertation, I describe how feminist thinkers and literary authors inspired me and made the writing possible. My yearning to change academic spaces to become inclusive of creative and reflexive writing was underpinned by the striving for embodied, dialogical, and emancipatory forms of knowledge in what was then my home discipline of social work. The situation I was struggling with was similar to what Richardson (1997: 289) describes from the viewpoint of sociology:

> Troubled with the ethical issues of doing research on other, I wrote about my own life. I did undo myself as I had done onto others. And, troubled by academic institutions, I began to discover more agreeable pedagogical and writing practices, and alternative community building sites.

I hope that this book will be a contribution to community building for sustainable situated writing characterised by equality and with the potential to de-hegemonise and intersectionalise writing (Livholts 2012a). I argue that by transforming textual forms and making use of in-between spaces, we can open up opportunities to explore the complexities of power relations in people's lives and disrupt the dominant sound of story-telling (cf. Hau'ofa 2008). As a situated writer, I have made use of theoretical conceptualisations as a politics of location and diffractive writing, *diffraktionsskrivande*. As a theory, diffraction constitutes a narrative prism for telling stories across geographical sites, bodies, and languages. As a method, diffractive writing sets the self into movement, through the artistic creation of textual and visual artefacts such as a professor's chair, snow angels, and the turbulence of water. An ethics of change requires giving attention to the multiple sites of power at work. It includes being gendered as 'woman' in different situations, writing in resistance to that name and at the same time carrying unearned privileges from sights and sites of whiteness. Writing through layers of whiteness brings with it a risk of reproducing dominance. As Cuesta and Mulinari (2018) show in a study of Swedish feminism and racism, at the level of embodied experiences, diversity and the politics of colour prevail within feminist collective contexts. The risk is that white feminists take on a 'good anti-racist' identity. Cuesta and Mulinari (2018: 13) warn that autoethnographic approaches in particular can lead to the risk that 'a subjective interpretation is translated and equalised into an understanding of power, body and place, at the risk of having an essentialist understanding of complex interactions'. Situated writing takes issues around power seriously and works in the intersections of privilege and marginalisation. The situated writer does not use the power of invisibility to speak from nowhere, but uses textual and visual shaping to learn about and challenge inequality through writing. To be situated as a writer involves a complex relationship between the personal and the political in the context of history and geopolitics. The embodied self, the collection of objects, items, images, memories, indoor and outdoor spaces, and landscapes are all parts of the shaping of the writing.

During the last few years, I have increasingly perceived my work on the untimely academic novellas as embarrassing, a self-portrait created through estrangement which, through the multiplicity of life stories over a long period of time, brings the unexpected into the present (Livholts 2018). This question of an ethics related to the local academic self has been re-actualised in the writing of this book. As I explained in the prologue, being granted funding for a sabbatical to write was unexpectedly emotionally ambivalent. I increasingly perceived writing as risky and ethically troublesome, in regard to both my own self and others. Reading Anzaldúa (1987: 65), I experienced a resonance with the depths and turbulences of the changing perceptions of self through writing, which is intimately intertwined with fears and vulnerability, but also resistance and belief in social change. She writes:

> She has this fear   that she has no names   that she has
> many names   that she doesn't know her names   She has
> this fear   that she's an image   that comes and goes clear-
> ing and darkening   the fear that she's the dreamwork inside
> someone else's skull   She has this fear   that if she takes off
> her clothes   shoves her brain aside peels off her skin   that
> if she drains   the blood vessels   strips the flesh from the
> bone   flushes out the marrow   She has this fear   that when
> she does reach herself   turns around to embrace herself   a lion's
> or witch's or serpent's head   will turn around swallow her and
> grin   She has this fear that if she digs into herself   she won't find
> anyone   that when she gets "there"   she won't find her notches
> on the trees   the birds will have eaten all the crumbs   She has
> this fear that she won't find the way back.

By wording and re-wording and the creating of in-between spaces in the textual shaping, Anzaldúa (1987) invites the reader to listen to and reflect upon the many fears that I read into the main concerns of an ethics of change and the self: the fears of being nameless, of losing the self, facing the self beyond recognition, and not finding the way back. Turning to the self with the intention of embracing the self, of finding the self, seems to be illusory and filled with uncertainty 'that she won't find the way back'. It was not until I wrote 'Writing Water' (Livholts 2013) that I could see how my life writing had influenced how I had lived my life.

Writing scholarly autobiography involves other people in the stories, who have often not been asked to participate with their lives. Ellis (2007) writes about the relational ethics involved in ethnographic and autoethnographic research, where the researcher is either friends with or knows the research participants, or is writing about family members. Feelings of anger may be evoked among people who feel that they are negatively represented or that they did not give permission to be portrayed. Readers may feel discomfort when reading about personal lives without knowing whether the person in the narrative gave permission.

> [...] autoethnography involves a back-and-forth movement between experiencing and examining a vulnerable self and observing and revealing the broader context of that experience. When we write about ourselves, we also write about others. In so doing, we run the risk that other characters may become increasingly recognizable to our readers, though they may not have consented to being portrayed in ways that would reveal their identity; or, if they did consent, they might not understand exactly to what they had consented. How do we honor our relational responsibilities yet present our lives in a complex and truthful way for readers?
>
> (Ellis 2007: 14)

My untimely academic novellas include writings and photographs of situations and relations with people in the university contexts where I have worked over the years, although no actual names are mentioned and the fictionalised style is protective towards recognition of specific persons. In regard to my family, I have removed names during the editing of the novellas for this book. *The Professor's Chair* (2010a) contains situations from my PhD studies. *The Snow Angel and Other Imprints* (Livholts 2010b) is a narrative that involves three generations of women, myself, my mother, and my grandmothers on both my father's and my mother's sides. *Writing Water* (2013) is a narrative in which I revisit the other two novellas and write about my life as a mother living with three sons, and the negative evaluation and rejection of my merits from the discipline to become a professor of social work.

As Ellis (2007) states, there is no one single answer to how we should practise relational ethics, but in the focus of interest, it is *a concern to care for*. A central epistemological ethical practice for me over the years has been to think about and decide: what can be written? Based on this question, I have chosen not to write about situations that I thought were too sensitive and to consider the ways in which the situation had broader implications at the institutional and societal levels from my point of view. I worked consciously to find what I thought was the best genre to write about my sons, and I communicated about what I wrote with them. Because they were at very different ages and a series of events and the publishing of the novellas further influenced our lives, these communicative acts of consent appear to be even more complex than if I had not asked for them. As Ellis (2007) states, it can be difficult to ask for permission after the writing is published, and to explain the reasons for writing in a way that involved a person in retrospect. At the same time, I don't believe that one can remove sensitive things even by not writing them. As Tamboukou (2015a) writes about analysing letters or diaries, analytically it is equally important for the reader to note the silences. I think this is particularly important to consider when using writing as a method employing diverse genres such as diaries, letters, and poetry, and indeed photographs. How do they speak to the reader? This is an open question.

I have written about people who were not alive at the time when I wrote about them, and this includes both my own memories of specific situations and stories told by my mother. To practise situated writing through intersections raises ethical concerns. For example, there are specific ways in which I write about my grandmothers, that when I read them now, appear to include sensitive aspects related to, for example, eating, embodiment, and conflicts. As I explain (Livholts 2013), my mother has been actively engaged in my work with the snow angel experiments and I have translated sections from that novella and read them to her. However, my writing in English means that she cannot read and respond to the ethics fully from her point of view.

The most difficult ethical questions have concerned writing about mothering and my sons. It is a fact that right from the time when I wrote my PhD dissertation and challenged academic genres of how a dissertation is supposed to be written, my life and the lives of my now adult children have been shaped by this (Livholts 2001/2011). In 'Writing Water' (2013: 179), I describe my intention as being to write through 'depths, waves, and turbulences, silences'. Beyond the negative judgement of my work from social work at that point, I re-situate my work in a 'community of dissident water writers'. When I write about 'water in the poetry lines', this is about love and tears, resistance to the norms of living a life as a family, and the challenges of moving between homes, universities, and schools. Page (2017: 28) calls for vulnerable writing:

> A vulnerable method does not attempt to resolve discomfort immediately through problem-solving, or by forms of sense making that utilise particular relational elements of cause and effect. Instead, what is at the heart of vulnerable methods and vulnerable writing are ongoing questions about what unsettles, about relations to the unfamiliar and strange, and about the erasure of the complexities of subjectivity when individuals and bodies and their actions do not fit or adhere to coherent themes of knowledge. This unsettled uncertainty of the research process, rather than foreclosing on further understandings, provides space for new forms of unknowing and continued attempts at understanding the stories of others.

What Page (2017) describes as vulnerable writing supports the framework that I call situated writing, with exemplars from my untimely academic novellas in this book. It is writing that is affirmative of the unexpected and the untimely, the messiness, gaps and silences, the slowness, the waiting rooms. bell hooks (1997, 1999) has addressed questions of ethics when writing autobiography and memoir: how multiple forms of oppression interact in family, education, writing, and publishing. In *Remembered Rapture: The Writer at Work*, hooks (1999: xi) invites the reader 'to share the dimensions of my writing life that take place behind the scenes'. Accountability and sustainability are intimately intertwined. Bränström Öhman (2010: 289) discusses hooks' genre-transgressive critical intersectional writing from the body as a lodestar for sustainable writing. This writing is characterised by simplicity, accessibility, and embodiment. Simplicity should not be mistaken for simple, but is an expression for the aim of making the complex clear. Accessibility is linked with narrativity beyond academic conventions to invite the reader into the story, and to write accessible and short sections that makes it possible for readers that cannot afford to buy the book, to read sections in the book shop. Embodiment is at the heart of feminist theorising, and it constitutes a key dimension of the writer at work; embodied, sited through memory and place, making use of writing as a form of lived inquiry. Situated writing actualises an ethics of change that is characterised by the complexity of the sustainability challenges faced by contemporary and future universities. Writing is at the heart of everyday academic practice, yet it is often treated as though there was only one form of writing suitable for all knowledge. As a consequence, the diversity and creativity that so many people bring when they enter academia is not considered a resource. Writing shapes knowledge. Writing shapes our many selves. What we see. Who we become.

Notes

1 This working strategy has developed over the years as a form of exhibiting textual and visual practices in my work on narratives of rape and masculinity (Livholts 2015d). For the writing of this section, I have been inspired by examples from the arts (see, for example, Nobel 2014), but also philology and history studies through Küster's (2016) work on writing and space, punctuation and emotions.
2 For a presentation of the memory work method as a situated and reflexive writing method, see also Livholts (2015b), in Livholts and Tamboukou (2015).
3 Elaine R. Hedges, Afterword to Gilman's (1892/2012) *The Yellow Wallpaper*. This afterword was written in 1973 (2012: 36).

Part II

A trilogy of untimely academic novellas

3   'The Professor's Chair'

I

The crouching fearful character, who had its home within the white walls of the corridors, was ready to announce its existence as a thinking*writing* subject.

Untimely?

Yes, indeed.

But necessary.

She leaned against the doorway. The warm palm of her hand rested against the smooth cool surface of wooden material.

It was a good spot for watching.

The red colour of the textile, which caressed along the outlines of the contours of the furniture, was attractive to the gaze.

Expensive cover; long high back; comfortable; easy to tilt.

Expensive cover.

Long high back.

Comfortable.

Easy to tilt.

*

Dear Maj,

I hope you endure my letters. At times, I am afraid that you will get too tired of listening to the endless problems that academe has brought to our lives. More than once I have been troubled by the thought that perhaps I should never have come here. This emotional uneasiness persistently stays with me no matter how hard I try to get rid of it. Indeed, academia can even be a fearful place. Did I send you the photograph of the building where my room is? I do not know why I began photographing, but began doing it when I worked on an experimental paper on memory work on the theme 'buildings of knowledge'. To be honest, I was shocked to find out that the place looks like a jail. I consider this proof of unhealthy environment and I am convinced it is deliberate architectural planning. I am convinced that the fact that I increasingly perceive myself as ugly is related to the place I am in.

Do you remember when I started as an assistant? By that time I had no intention of making an academic career. On the contrary, I was put off by the fact that the professor at the department had that title. Already by that time, I felt that there was something wrong with me for thinking this way. Nevertheless, now comes the obscure and difficult part for you to read. A persistent thought has taken root in my mind and I cannot get rid of it even in my sleep. I want to become a professor! What do you think? I would not dare to say this to you over the phone, because I am afraid that you would have advised me not to – before you have considered the idea thoroughly! However, I will give you a few reasons why. There is no doubt that I will be able to qualify academically in research and teaching, and the important thing is that I will not have to give up my capacity to write. I have discovered it is the format and language that is crucial for making a career! The way academics write provides the basic ground for creating collective belonging and identity. However, I will not be able to accomplish this without your help. It is true that academic life may cause serious illness. Therefore, I ask you if you would consider being my mentor in the unethical and therefore improper, but necessary, project which I have in mind – to become a professor. Please respond as soon as you have considered my question carefully.

Yours Sincerely,

Mona

P.S. I think about the title as a chair. At least I will have a long-term employment after all these years. It will be good for me and the children. I might even get rid of my ugly face.

II

She had fallen in disgrace with time. It was obvious that she had no confidence in the way people around her used the concept of time; this had brought confusion, but also playfulness and the unexpected to her life. Out of sight and reach she was placed in the transparency and invisibility of the very same body – her own – where time and space had other, yet unknown meanings. Now she entered the room, unnoticed, and found herself sitting quietly in front of him while he spoke incessantly. The front side of her body revealed nothing about the intense activity going on, did not speak of someone with a mind full of fantasy and liveliness. Her arms were hanging loosely down, as if they had been too poorly attached to the shoulders; the straight posture reinforced the impression of a very slim physique. She wore bright-coloured clothes, and the heart-shaped face was framed by thin blond hair. Her hands were cupped around the somewhat rough and unpleasant surface of the seat of the visitors' chair she was sitting on; the fingertips tapped the edge below the seat with small regularly movements.

The drumming of a silent orchestra.

Without notice.

Unnoticed.

He was a well-formed product of his time, sitting, leaning slightly forward, in his chair. His mouth moved continuously, but since he had no talent for speech, his words came out in jerks. His body confirmed that he was under pressure through the twitching of his chest and upper body. It was an allegory of a conductor without a baton – as if he had been misplaced; out of place. A desk dominated the space between them. Papers were spread all over it; white papers, letters, black signs which had been crossed by a red pen that marked his thinking on her writing. She was already mourning the loss behind the curtains of right and wrong, true and false. But at the same time she was relieved from guilt for visiting so many places while taking supervision. It was impolite, even rude not to pay attention to what he said, but excursions were necessary – she had to try to keep her spirit up. She sought excitement and challenge to the mind, but found that she had come to the wrong place; that she was forced to adapt her thinking and writing to industrial mechanical production, where tools of the unseen were used to cut and shape, sharpen and polish. This provided safety to power; sameness. She, in the name of science, had fallen into disgrace with time.

She glanced at the chair he was sitting in.

Long high back; comfortable.

The Professor's Chair.

III

Hot sun. No wind. They sat on the built-in balcony at lunch time. Every room, every corner, in as well as outdoors, was full of people. Students sat, lay, and leaned against each other on the grass together with books, papers, bags, sandwiches, and cool drinks. The mumbling of voices spread pleasantly over the campus area. It was during this time essays were written both day and night, bodies aching from the hard work of thinking and writing, and parties replaced each other. Fantastic plans of a successful future coexisted with anxiety of the unknown and fear of failure.

The future.

Unseen.

All of a sudden, the cynic and the tragic presented themselves, and brought some coolness to the moment of heat. The conversation at the table was about tenured positions at the department. It was in that moment she spoke, simply stated honestly from her heart how depressing it was to go to work every day and find that all tenured positions were held by men, that so much influence, decision making and resources were given to men. One of the professors answered that, unfortunately, this was the case and that it would take at least a hundred years to change this. She answered him so suddenly and straightforwardly that she was surprised.

'I will be dead by then!'

A simple and very brief statement in that moment.

Silence.

No condolences.

He saw no responsibility to provoke change. She had no future in the hands of professors or others with power in the department, only by what she herself could accomplish, and not even then. She realised that time itself is the main actor; time brings coffee and sandwiches, distributes money, holds speeches, decides salaries, and invites speakers. Time is the voice that speaks through the roughness of structure – 'I am sorry, this is how things are!' She wants out of the category of 'women' in this time, and she wants to dedicate her mind to intellectual work. But his speech forces slowness to her movements. A sense of tiredness, almost sleepiness, shadows her abilities, her senses. She will be dead in a hundred years.

Untimely, isn't it?

Deported to the room of silence, cut off from the continuous conversation at the table, she becomes aware of the movable image in the window glass of herself and her colleagues. But they were not the only ones sitting there! Beside them, in a circle, a group of women sat on the cold concrete floor with their legs crossed. Text strips were attached over their eyes and mouths. She was terrified when she saw them and wondered if it was the past or the future which presented themselves in this way. Or, even more upsetting, death! She thought she had seen, if not dead, rejected, silenced, expelled women, and she asked herself if this would happen to her as well. Would she join the circle of ignored, run down, invisible women? If so, the next generation would be forced to pass through so many women's bodies and lives during all the hundred years to finally become professors.

Landscape of offices.

Locked up.

Colorlessness.

Squareness.

She wobbled in her step. The walls moved. All of a sudden she was not walking down the straight and broad corridor, but a narrow and winding path. She finds her room under the pressure of great strain, enters the door, and touches the chest and the stomach in search of her breath. Someone has put on a too tight bandage around her chest. It is difficult to breathe.

Hunting hare and she is guard in the darkness and silence of the night.

Burning grass; she breathes spring and moves as fast as the whimsical wind.

The rhythmic movements of the horse running and sound of clattering hoofs.

The smell of dust.

A fox screaming.

She is woken up by her own scream. Looks in despair for her hands. Cannot turn on the light without hands! Rolls out of bed and hit her knees hard towards the floor and then the elbows; a shooting pain searches her head. She manages to reach the hallway where a soft light from the street leaks in, which makes it possible to examine her hands. They hang loosely along the body. She can hardly move them and suffers from a stinging pain. But she finds no visible marks and returns to her bed; shivering she lies awake, upset and shocked, and asks herself – is it worth it? But in that very moment she realises that the question is wrongly put. She cannot waste any time. She has only twenty years left. Much less than a hundred years. But she can hardly write at the same time as seconds become months and turn into years and sickness is the only time offered to her.

One hour later, she is sitting in bed holding a cup of hot tea in the same hands that she recently lost. Feeling the heat.

*

Dear Maj,

I have settled in at the cottage and this is my first evening here; I feel delighted and harmonious! The people who rent it were rather irritated that they had to move out at the end of June. In a way, I can understand their frustration, but I simply told myself that it is, after all, my cottage even though I cannot afford to leave it uninhabited during winter. This spring I have decided to work with analysis which fits well into established international journals. Right now, I have an article waiting to be published in Feminist Theory. You have a reason to be proud of me. There is a lot of competition to be published there! And did I tell you I have also published an article in a Swedish Academic Journal of Women's Studies? I know it sounds a bit crazy, but perhaps we should celebrate already at this stage? What if we find ourselves with no reason to celebrate if I never become professor? I know, forbidden thinking, which takes me nowhere and does no good. I sometimes think I may have underestimated my sensitivity to adjustment to academic life, even though my goal is obvious. Did I tell you I have joined a feminist writing group at the university? I have showed the Professor's Chair and received positive feedback. But I have not yet showed them my letters to you. I hope they allow them to remain in the text so that they will be made public, to a wider audience, once the book is finished. Now it is time to write and work. I have two texts I need to finish. One is my 'old' study about media report on rape (which makes me feel so uneasy and sometimes even afraid when I work on it). I also have to finish an article about the process of writing among academic feminists who have written something within another genre. To be honest, both these studies are demanding to write. However, now I continue working reassured that you are always beside me to support me.

Summer greetings,

Love, Mona

IV

She pulled the green and red checked blanket along the grass in the late afternoon sun. She had been lying at the water's edge, accompanied by the reassuring rhythm of the waves, reading a considerable number of articles and at the same time enjoying the warm rays from the sun. It was getting cooler, and she turned away from the increasingly distant beams of comfort as she began walking towards the wooden cottage, which seemed to be glowing with dark yellow colours in the light. The manuscript 'The Professor's Chair' had to be finished before she left. The two women in the text had begun to live their own lives. It had become almost impossible to differentiate between memories, auto-biographical writing, and fiction. The consequence was that she had developed a habit of watching the slim woman character in the novella at a distance; out of respect; discomfort or even dislike. At the same time as she was concerned about the loss of visionary thinking and cynism that the letter-writer seemed to express. And what was more, the story had started to lay great demands on her around the clock. She no longer found a place for rest. Her mind was speeding and intrigued by her own thinking. This created demands to straighten up her body, keep the goal in sight, and ignore every tendency to feel sick and disoriented.

She pulled herself back to the spectacular view of the smooth reflecting surface of the water and the cottage painted orange by the sunset. She focused and returned to the structure and rhythm of the text in the articles, to the performance of a grand narrative; unheard; no sound. By squatting she is able to touch the surface, plunge her fingers into the water, be embraced by the black material at the same time as she forces it to move, a temporal disturbance of the rhythmic movements. She pushes her hand beneath the surface and moves it intensely around like a ladle in loose dough mixture. The water offers resistance, tries to regain control of the rhythm which she has interrupted, and will soon slow down her movements. She has now succeeded in transforming the water into a funnel. The funnel of an eye. She keeps going, and the second eye helps her to see straight into the muddy material at the bottom of the lake. Interestingly, the circle of women sitting together, holding each other's hands, appears again. But since the surface of the water is constantly moving, what she sees does not scare her as last time. This is a much more pleasant scene. They are moving.

Thoughts; memories; fragments of thinking.

At the same time as the future cannot be foreseen, it has become a thought that touches everything and pulled her in a condition of movement without direction. It is at that very moment, the mumbling of voices, which can hardly be heard, makes her listen very carefully. She puts the ear against the planks, holds her breath, waits. Now it is time to reject written words which claim to have no author; it is time to invite the living.

V

She came in through one of the main buildings at the university, walked through the cafeteria, went up the elevator, and was about to enter through the last glass door to the department. It was so heavy that she had to put down both her bags to be able to open it. It was at that moment she laid eyes on it; the professor's chair was placed at the end of the corridor tunnel. She peered in, trying to work out if it had a note attached to it, but could not be sure from this distance. When she was close enough, she reached out and touched the cloth with her finger tips. Surprisingly, a piece of paper is attached to it with the word 'storeroom' written on it, a tragic place for unwanted university furniture.

A smell of dust.

The color of greyness.

She was convinced that the chair really would be placed in the store room, looked at the yellow note, and considered the situation. Now was the time to get hold of a chair for someone who really needed one, and who would need it more than she did?

Abundance.

Somewhere to sit.

Gratefulness and humbleness.

Privileges.

Hands which take hold of.

Holding hands.

Waves.

The unfearful.

*

Dear Maj,

This letter begins with a somewhat solemn declaration/it is soon time for the guests to be invited. The red sofa has arrived and is very decorative in its place in the living room! I am actually sitting in it when I am writing this letter to you. The cushions are soft; they feel more wonderful than I could imagine. I really look forward to your arrival! It is finally time to celebrate! Because the new sofa arrived I took the opportunity to rearrange the furniture and I placed the lovely mirror in a nice spot opposite of the sofa. I can actually see myself this very moment of writing. It is impossible to say if it is the red cloth that makes the color of my hair so central. As you know I have always envied you your blond hair, but after a successful dying my own boring rat color has a warm dark brown luster. You will like it.

I feel content. Not happy. But pleased. After all I have reached my goal to achieve a position which pays reasonably well. And I must say, and this may sound a bit narcissistic, but I think I look good, at least better than before. I think it has to do with my posture.

At the same time, I worry about my health. I suffer from terrible nightmares about women who have their eyes and mouths covered by some kind of tape. And during the last month I sometimes hear a peculiar sound from the bedroom where I keep the chair which I brought home from the department. To be honest I actually stole it and had to make up a lie to my colleagues that I had never seen it in the corridor. The odd thing is that I took it in full daylight when I arrived early one morning. Universities can be the emptiest spaces and this particular morning and I have to say it was indeed timely! But to continue to tell you about the peculiar sound from the room, I cannot help going there to investigate what the sound really is. The worst thing is that every time I do so I am struck by an intense feeling that someone has visited and just left. I need you to search through the room when you arrive. As a matter of fact one could think that not only myself, but even other people think the room is interesting. At this very moment, as I write to you, a man is standing outside the window and staring into the bedroom. Totally unembarrassed! Well I guess that is one of the disadvantages of living on the ground floor. People can actually look straight in. I need to use the curtains more. What should I do without you? There is no one else I can share the uneasiness of emotions that life has brought. Looking forward to talking to you face to face soon!

Love,

Mona

In the soft greenish light of the lamp, he watches a woman. What he sees is the appearance of an unlikely character; a thin body with long arms moves quickly and a bit twitchy; a humanised shadow. He is caught by the decisiveness he is witnessing through her movements. But all of a sudden they become slow. She reaches out to the bookshelf, and her fingers touch each and every one of the books in a row before she finally picks one and sits down in a red chair in front of the desk. Now the only visible sign of her presence is part of her blond hair sticking up above the chair. Without noticing he had slowed his movements down, passing the house and the window on the ground floor. He can see how she uses the chair as a vehicle for moving between the desk and the bookshelf again.

Each time she firmly put down her feet and make a push, the wheels of the chair make a low sighing sound against the soft plastic floor. She leans comfortably against the high soft back.

Expensive cover; long high back; comfortable; easy to tilt.

Expensive cover.

Long high back.

Comfortable.

Easy to tilt.

Professor's Chair.

Figure 3.1 University building. Author's photograph. Sweden, 2005.

4 'The Snow Angel and Other Imprints'

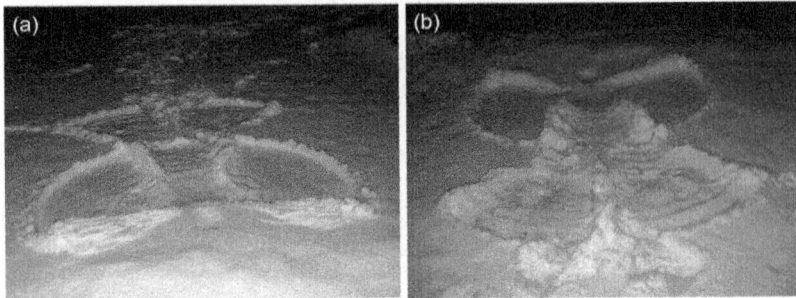

Figure 4.1 (a and b) Evening snow angels. Author's photograph. Sweden, 2008.

I

She is lying on the frozen ground, embraced by soft, dry
powdery snow.
Face touches sky.
Arms and legs spread out.
The language of folding cloth marks a temporal figure.
Carefully rise to upstanding position,
Hold balance and step out of the imprint,
Watch the contours of a Snow Angel.

Snow beneath her jacket; a miniature stream of water is running
down her neck.
Changing form and silently disappearing.

She chooses a good spot for watching.
Seeing her self and another through greyish camera reality.

A bodily imprint; white on white.
Creating of the timely; dissolvable by time.
Translations of body and landscape.

20th May, 2008

Dear Maj,

It looks like I have soon reached a desirable goal in my academic career, associate professor. The professor at the department supports my application for promotion and last week I sent it to the board at the university. Now follows a period of waiting, while an expert reader makes a judgment of my academic work. Ironically, at the same time as I am about to reach a long-desired position, I nourish doubts about the meaning of making a career. While I thought that reaching this goal would help me to navigate through the academic terrain, and even offer me some feeling of homeness, the emotions I encounter are confusion and a desire for change. However, what this desire for change means is unclear. My academic life seems to be a story about someone who I watch from a distance. What I see is a woman academic who grew up on a farm in a wooded county, a girl who always wanted to leave home and seek a future somewhere else, and who has continued to live through that yearning for another future. But my restless mind keeps troubling me in adult life. When I moved to this new university two years ago, I decided to organise my life in five-year plans, convinced that this feeling of not-belonging would take me to yet another place in due time. However, at the moment I write these words to you, I realise that writing is a more powerful practice than I had foreseen. I suspect I won't leave this place. Not because someone forces me to stay, but because I have begun to feel a warm, almost loving, attachment to it. This emotion is most striking in the mornings when I leave my house and am met by the view of the lake and the sound of the water, and when I walk from the parking lot to the university building where I work; in particular, during dark winter mornings, when fires in black iron posts welcome me. I actually believe that it is the water and the snow, the landscape outside the university walls that will make me stay. However, as my letters to you have shown through the years, academia can be a frightful place, potentially threatening for women's health. A common expression for illness here is to 'walk into the wall'. Was that what happened to me when I was a doctoral student accompanied by the human shadow in the white corridors at the university? Just as it was then, writing is my way of resisting bad health. Hope to talk to you soon, take care,

Love, Mona

II

Some windows allow more sight than others. Her grandmother's window was designed as a triangle, bravely sticking out from the brick body of the house. In her early teenage years, she spent a lot of time in her grandmother's flat and would often sit by the window, and watch.

Watching silence.

There was not much to see, yet sameness seemed to be a very good starting point for imagination. Outside the window, a few narrow streets formed a cross-road. To the left stood some older wooden houses and to the right, light grey block buildings with red balconies. The design and language of these buildings were quite different. It was through that window her thoughts about the world were shaped; images that allowed her to travel when travelling was not possible; fantasies, which made it possible to move in space and time and still being secretly in love with the landscape of rural space; rejecting what she then thought of as the old-fashioned, farming space. A popular TV series from the U.S. inspired plans for a future occupation as a lawyer. By the age of nineteen, she got so far as applying to one of Sweden's most highly ranked universities, but changed her mind when the acceptance letter arrived. She did not think she was bright enough, and it was too big of a financial investment. Instead, she applied for social work studies, a profession with shorter education. Her stepfather complained; studying was worthless. What she did not know then was that the Sunday kitchen table was an excellent place to practice and develop rhetorical skills. Her grandmother, who was a working-class woman in her fifties with bad health already, would challenge her stepfather in a verbal battle about politics and social injustice. She was a social democrat, and he was voting for the right wing party. Even though the atmosphere would sometimes be very strained, due to strong disagreements, she liked Sundays and her grandmother's visit more than anything else.

Despite the fact that the farming life where she was brought up provided her with good financial security, she identified with her grandmother and her mother; one lived under economic and social restraint, and the other with economic security, but under the control and disobedience of a man. Some of the most vivid memories she had as an adult were some of the stories told by her mother about her grandmother. One story was based on the situation when her grandmother was eighteen and had her first child (her mother). She lived in a village and needed to take herself and her child to another village.

To be able to bring the newborn child with her, she used a paper box. Although this was nothing she had witnessed, she had a very clear image in her mind about how it all happened. She saw before her how her grandmother had tried, perhaps with blankets or other soft material, to make the box as comfortable as possible. How she had pushed the bike with one hand and at the same time balanced the vehicle between the trees and roots on the path. There was also another story, told by her mother and grandmother, which involved her own birth. The story was that when she was born, she was as tiny as a bag of flour. Her mother, who was nineteen years old, cried.

> *A large woman eating on a small plate.*
> *A child in a box,*
> *and a child as tiny as a bag of flour.*

III

30th November, 2008

I am visiting my mother a few weeks before Christmas. I have brought the camera, eager to take photographs of the first snow. I have also planned to make snow angels. My mother knows that I am writing the second untimely academic novella in a trilogy and that I intend to use the symbol of a snow angel to reconstruct parts of my life history for analytical purposes. Nevertheless, I feel embarrassed when she is present and watching me laying down in the snow on the lawn to make snow angels. It is evening and when I lay on the ground, I become award of the darkness above and around me. The snow is heavy, wet, 'tösnö', and really good for making snowmen. It is not the kind of snow I would have made snow angels with, if I hadn't been working on my untimely academic novella. However, I know that it may not be possible to make snow angels tomorrow if the temperature increases. I am a bit worried about photographing in the darkness, not knowing if the camera will be able to visualise what I see. It turns out that what the camera sees is something quite different than I expected. Both my mother and I react towards the distinct imprint that the angel makes on the snow and how the darkness constitutes a powerful framing. The angel though is not white, but greyish, and it is possible to see nuances of green grass through the imprint. It is also obvious that I have no memory of a snow angel with a head. My imprint of a snow angels this late evening on my mother's lawn leaves a clear round mark of a head; it is a head separated from the body, and the body seems huge in perspective. This snow angel has no similarities with memories of making snow angels when I was a child. In my memories, making a snow angel was a playful performance, an imprint of white on white, the beauty of an artistic creation, but always temporary; eroding before my eyes if the wind was strong and the snow dry and light or day by day depending on the weather.

A bodily imprint; white on white.

Creation of the timely; dissolvable by time.

Performative translations of landscape.

15th December, 2008

Dear Maj,

It has been snowing for almost a week. It is the most beautiful winter in several years; however, it has been very untimely, interrupted by my stepfather's illness. Last Sunday when I was at home clearing the flat, the phone rang. It was my sister who told me that she and my mother were in town because my stepfather was in the hospital; he was seriously ill, and it was uncertain if he would survive. As you know I have never had a close relationship with him, but one characterised by conflicts and disappointments. That phone call did not only introduced discomfort and problems, it was like opening the curtains at a theatre where I, my mother, and my sisters were the main characters. The reason that I had this strong feeling of drama probably had to do with the events that proceeded him entering in to the hospital, and also the power he always had to run my mother's and my sister's lives. It was snowing and very windy the night he came to the hospital for intensive care. He had been lying for days naked in his bed while his house became colder and colder; his fingers and toes were turning blue and his tongue developed deep cracks caused by dehydration. Ever since I heard about it for the first time, it has been on my mind, like a film played again and again. However, while the doctors were trying to save his life and two of my sisters and my mother patiently took turns watching over him for several days, I went to work. Routinely I went past the iron bowl filled with fire every morning, came inside the house, went up the stairs, unlocked the door to my room and turned on the computer. What had changed was that the daily routine was followed by a specific awareness. Despite the fact that I love my mother and my sisters, I was ambivalent about their presence. Was I guarding who I have become since I left 'them'? Another unexpected consequence was that my stepfather's unconsciousness made it possible for me to speak to him during the brief visits I made; for the first time in my life as far as I could remember, I talked to him and I touched his arm, his cheek. Touching challenged anger and distance; and the feeling of being a character in a play pursued me late at nights; I was ambivalent to the changes. My mother said to me that during one of her visits, she told him that I had applied for associate professor. She was not sure if he could hear her or understood what it meant. 'It is a sign that you have done well though', she said. It occurred to me that no one in the family I come from, apart from one of my sisters, knows what my work is about. Perhaps I should not blame them. How can my mother tell her friends that her daughter is soon to be an associate professor and is making snow angels as part of an ongoing project? As you may already have gathered from my letters, the more I write, the more I learn that the problem of unhomeyness is more complex than I could imagine.

Love, Mona

IV

Gurli Grundin had created a name for herself as a skilful handcrafter in the area and made a living out of it. Her mother had told her that Gurli, who was her distant grandmother on her father's side, had been married three times and had six children.

It was an amazing coincidence that the first day when she began her apprenticeship at the local newspaper, only fourteen years old, the journalist told her that she was going to accompany him to interview a woman who owned a popular handicraft shop. From his perspective, she was just a pupil on a weekly practice. He did not know that the woman whom they were going to interview this afternoon was her grandmother; and she said nothing. They arrived at a white house situated near the main road. A small red building, the handicraft shop, had been built in a very different style from the other houses to mark the traditional colours of houses in the landscape, red and white. As soon as they stepped out of the car, the door to the house opened and a woman came out. She smiled and gave them a warm welcome. She passed as 'the pupil', and together with the journalist, she followed her grandmother who took them for a guided tour of her house and the handicraft shop. She entered rooms with wooden floors and photographs everywhere; photographs on shelves, tables, and the piano. No photos of her. In a small room, she saw a black desk and a chair – a place that looked like an office. It was indeed unexpected to have a guided tour by her own grandmother, whom she had never met previously and who did not recognise her. Still she did not reveal her identity, but when they were about to leave, she suddenly introduced herself as 'Mona, your grandchild'. The elderly woman with the heart-shaped face and round cheeks looked at her with surprise and joy and said: 'Are you really my grandchild? Why did you not say anything?' She embraced her and held her at an arm's length and said: 'You look thin. You must come and visit me soon'. Next winter holiday she spent a week at her grandmother's house. She walked across the floors that she once had been told that her mother had scrubbed; she looked at the photographs and was told some of the history of the faces, and each day she admired the black desk and the chair; a working space for a woman. She also spent time in the handicraft shop and was introduced to customers as 'Mona, my grandchild, Pelle's daughter'. It was the only time she spent with her grandmother while she was alive.

V

17th January, 2009

It is afternoon, around three o'clock. It is cold and I have dressed well on my way out for my regular walk around the mountain. The camera lies in the pocket of my jacket. I think that I live in the most beautiful landscape. The county has a particular dramatic and powerful character, situated inland (which is thought of not as good as the coastal area) with hills, forest, and a big lake, and often in the winter a lot of snow and wind. It is a small city divided into two parts: the mainland and an island. During my mountain walk, I have planned to make snow angels and to photograph them for my project. I notice that the sun is down and that I need to photograph before I go for the walk or it will be too dark. I look for a spot. I would like to find one where no one can see me, but there are houses everywhere. I choose a spot near the lake. I am more enthusiastic this time than at my mother's house because the snow is dry, soft and powdery, and deeper. I try to relax and fall back. I hear a dull sound when I land on my back. I stretch out my arms and legs and begin to do the rhythmic movements. I see branches of trees reaching up towards the blue sky. It is comfortable; all of a sudden, I am struck by how tired I feel. For some reason, I think of a woman whom I met at a conference a few years ago. She had a high position as a leader within her culture. When I met her, she spoke about how she had learned to stand being bullied at work by her chief. The next time I heard about her was when I read in the newspaper that she had resigned. She was cited saying that when she was on vacation she swam in the ocean and a turtle appeared. It was during that moment when she had eye contact with the turtle that it was clear to her that she could not continue to do what she was doing.

I stand up and start photographing. I try to lean over the imprint of the snow angel to get as clear a shot as possible. Looking at the photographs, I am struck by the light. It is definitely not white, but blue. The photography changes my perspective, and the colour of blue follows me during my walk around the mountain.

> Seeing another through bluish camera reality.
> Imprint.
> Embodiment of whiteness, a temporal figure.

25th February, 2009

Dear Maj,

I am writing this letter to you feeling slightly more content than I have been lately. It will soon be time to celebrate my promotion to associate professor. The department has invited everyone to a feast and in the invitation they have mentioned that we are also celebrating that I and a colleague now have this title. However, I have also had some odd reactions when I expressed my goal to become a full professor, in particular from women academics. Some would say nothing and the words I just spoke disappeared as though consumed by a third, invisible party. Other would act as if I had insulted them, and began to speak about how much they valued their family life. 'My family is most important for me and comes first, then my career!' The most difficult expression to interpret is those who laugh or even say 'You are funny!' I have given up trying to understand what they mean by it. Isn't it interesting that this week the university is arranging a whole day about careers for women in higher education? And I heard from a friend that the deputy vice chancellor had spoken on the radio and said that if universities are going to change the current situation, with so few women professors, there is a need for special measures. I am very interested to see what they are going to do. There is no doubt that statistics concerning women professors are depressing reading. In Sweden, approximately 18 percent of all professors are women and at my university the percentage is even lower. The other day I sat in a meeting with a group for equality at the university. We were meeting in a colleague's office, and she had written the names of the academics who were now in the process of becoming associate professors and professors on a white board. Among these names I saw my own and as I watched I felt how the reports on equality became a heavy burden on my legs. I realized how much work I had put into committees and boards and meetings all these years and I know I could not go on in the same way anymore. I felt like I was a silent witness to the documented inequalities of this time, fostered by the statistics to know my place. On the other hand, an intriguing question is whether my previous name, Scheffer Kumpula, would have been among the names on that board? Livholts is an invented name. Did I invent privilege? The moment brought a wave of memories to me and I felt like a very old woman who had no energy to cross that last line for promotion to professor. I actually decide to leave the group and the board and to try to reach the professor's chair despite the fact that I know that the odds may be worse than I imagined. I can see my own shadow lurking to guide me in the wrong direction, doomed to a life within the statistical barriers. I need to get away from this place and I have decided to travel to see you in May; do you think that would be possible?

Love, Mona

VI

People passed now and then. She noticed, no rather, she analysed their appearance. She read facial expressions, interpreted body languages, clothes, ages, social interaction; individuals. Couples, groups; distanced, holding hands, touching. They passed; she watched them, like a thief, cheaply stolen lives from strangers passing in the street; viewing the scene from the restaurant behind the coloured glass wall. Watching. She knew she had no access to the truth. She did not believe it existed at all. In the process of becoming researcher, she had developed an analytical eye. Or had it always been there, since childhood?

> A correcting voice.
> A resisting thought.
> Thoughts of resistance.

Mirroring herself in the darkness of the glass wall and the murmuring floor, she saw a middle-aged woman in a black skirt and a golden-brown sweater wearing silver jewellery; a blond middle-aged woman with a disturbing red nose beneath her makeup because she had not protected herself properly from the merciless beams of the Australian sun. Glass and murmur; she could still hear the ocean; smell and visualise the seaweed and the salt, admiring the brown stones with wrinkles.

Solitude.
Browsing, rearing, smashing, clicking, silence,
capsulated in a room of silence, stones with wrinkles.

Imagine myself, the author, in a pose of translation; holding, sitting, reading, thinking about the story written by Charlotte Perkins Gilman, *The Yellow Wallpaper*. Feel my emotions of eagerness, enthusiasm, and fearful interpretations; notice the characteristically dusty air; observe the creature breathing depression in the back of my neck. Follow me to the landscapes of misunderstandings; to the outfit of misfit belongings; to the writing of too late invitations to a guest that will never come. Listen to the voice of the older woman academic who tells me that the book I just read was written more than a hundred years ago. Have I lost track of time (?) she asks and reminds me that the book is set in a different time and place from now.

Misunderstandings.
Translations.
Too late.

Foot prints.
Landscape of stones.
Cracks; patterns.
Transparency of first ice.
Imprints of an untimely author.

We have now transferred to the time of pebbles underneath my shoes, to the time when grey was the authority in life and I began to register even the smallest sound. You may publish the diary, he says; it is really fine for you to write about us if it helps, and it is alright with me if you wish to publish it. That was the last commitment he gave, a permission to publish grief over lost love. They were an academic couple, the kind of relationship that, through the years, she had resisted to engage in. To her surprise she learned through the short and intense relationship that it helped make her feel that she was in the right place. Four years later, she decides to set herself in a mode of translation. She reads the whole diary, more than fifty pages of text, written on the computer late at night. Reading about her own grief scares her. His promise haunts her. The relationship with him caused a disruption in her life, in the rhythm of everyday and working life.

> Untimely love.
> Leaving the place where they fell in love.
> You may publish the diary he says.
> Untimely promise.
> Full stop.

It is windy when the plane lands at the airport in Northern Sweden. She arrives after two-and-a-half years of absence, invited to present her research at a workshop and a seminar. She had decided not to present the paper 'The Snow Angel and Other Imprints'. Instead, she chose an article that was already in print. Recently, a stream at a conference which had accepted the Snow Angel paper had been cancelled. The organizer explained that there was not enough interest for the stream and advised her to present her paper in one of the other streams. It became increasingly difficult to write. She switched languages and tried writing in Swedish, thinking it was her poor English that was the problem, but soon discovered this was not the case. It was the topic and the untimely connections. The delayed arrivals and untimely promises.

30th May, 2009

Dear Maj,

I wanted to thank you for a wonderful weekend. I loved our long conversations, the promenades and the delicious meals. As always when I leave, I feel that I would like to have the kind of place that you have, a beautiful house in the countryside; at the same time I am caught in-between worlds and have almost given up on the idea that I will be able to create a space for myself that feels like home. When I moved here I decided that furniture like bookshelves and hangers should not be attached to the walls so they could easily be moved. The bookshelves at work though are firmly attached to the walls and I think that the shelves in my office represents not only titles of ongoing research projects, but me, who I am, what my life is. One shelf is for my research on the telephone as a meeting place, one for media studies on rape and one for untimely academic novellas. And I just realized that I need one for the anthology project for the book on innovative forms of writing research. The department is a good place for me to work most of the time, however, in Sweden scholarly belonging is important and I am a misfit. Even though I have my degree in social work, my schooling is interdisciplinary. I also belong to gender studies, and at the same time to none of these disciplines. As you know I have begun to create a new academic space by founding a network for reflexive academic writing methodologies, which I coordinate. I am grateful that my idea was supported by the vice chancellor and I am really inspired by the communication with members. I nourish a hope that the network will show me the way to a future in academia. I have organized several conferences already. This summer I look forward to travelling to an autobiography conference where I will present a text I am writing right now. It is called 'The Snow Angel and Other Imprints'. I plan to include some of my letters to you. I have been encouraged by my sons who say that they want to read about that woman who struggles with finding an identity and a home in the snow angel text. Today I sent my oldest son two photographs from the promotion to Associate Professor. He thought that the one that shows when I received the certificate is nice and I enclose it with this letter for you to see. There is also another photograph, which includes all five academics (including me) who were awarded the promotion; three women and two men. It is promising from the perspective of statistics. What interests me, though, are the life stories of academics and I actually think that my interest has provided me with extra hearing skills. Recently I set up a book corner in the corridor outside my room. Among these books, I feel I belong. I actually think that sometimes I can hear the voices of the authors. I have begun to write some of them down and have created 'the R.A.W. wall of citations' in the hallway at the department. I hope you can come and visit the exhibition. I am afraid that the cleaning staff will remove it before summer.

Love, Mona

VII

She is lying on the frozen ground, embraced by soft, dry
powdery snow.
Face touches sky.
Arms and legs spread out.
The language of folding cloth marks a temporal figure.
Carefully rise to upstanding position,

Hold balance and step out of the imprint,
Watch the contours of a Snow Angel.

She chooses a good spot for watching.
Seeing her self and another through bluish camera reality.

It is cold. The temperature is below fifteen degrees. When the man passes the harbour, he sees someone lying in the deep snow with arms and legs spread out. What is that person doing lying still in the snow this cold afternoon by itself? It is difficult to get a clear view, and he walks the path near the lake to get a closer look. He can clearly see that it is a woman with a white jacket and black pants with trainers on her feet. She has pulled up the hood, probably to protect her neck from the snow and the coldness. All of a sudden, she begins to do rhythmic movements by moving her arms and legs, and he realises that she is making a snow angel. After walking a short distance, he looks back and sees how the woman rises to standing position, brings a camera from her pocket, and photographs her own bodily imprint. He is fascinated to see that the whole scene is embedded in a distinct blue light.

Creating of the timely; dissolvable by time.
Translations of body and landscape.

Watch the contours of a Snow Angel.

5   'Writing Water'

Figure 5.1 Water. Author's photograph. Sweden, 2011.

Had it not been too late

Nobody has anywhere succeeded for very long in containing knowledge. Knowledge seeps through institutions and structures like water through the pores of a membrane. Knowledge seeps in both directions, from science to society as well as from society to science. It seeps through institutions and from academia to and from the outside world (Nowotny 2008: 1).

Had it not been too late, I would have claimed I am
writing water,
In the age of untimeliness.
The letter is sent too soon, too late.
The recipient has moved.

Written in the layers of ice, cracks, breaking the line,
Had it not been too late,
I would have claimed that I am writing water.

Through all uncountable years of metaphoric captivity
I was always writing water;

but it was just now when you were leaving with the train and
the lake threw rain on our faces,
that I was astonished to know this.

It was the most snow-poor autumn for the last hundred years in
Sweden, and 'Writing Water' had developed as a story that claimed
existence in its own right. She was an untimely novella writer based in
a northern peripheral location in world terms, and writing water was
a forceful activity. In the North Pole, the ice was melting, and in other
parts of the world, drought forced people to move and caused deaths
in a world of unequal resources. Floods and storms, hurricanes, and
earthquakes could be devastating, particularly in areas with poorly
built houses. Water also had a health-promoting effect for human life,
an artful creation, a source for recreation, the beauty of stillness, the
sound of waves, and the endless colour richness. In the process of writing, she noted that human beings consisted of seventy per cent water,
equal to the amount of water on earth.

'Writing Water' emerged originally from her fascination and fear of
water. During the years 2002–2007, she wrote a book about serial rape
that had water in the title (Livholts, 2007). Eventually she had begun
to live near water. When she moved to rural space to live and work
at a new university in 2006, her flat was situated 100 metres from the
lake. During these years, she developed a specific relationship to this
inland lake; its shifting colours of greyish, bluish and blackish; the
brownish stone landscape below the surface; the glimmering moon-
light reflection in the surface that created a pathway between earth
and heaven. Once she allowed herself to feel the rhythms of the water
in her bodily senses, movement occurred from within. The surface, as
blank as the organs that kept her body alive, kept her heart beating.

However, the forceful character of writing water was also intimately bound up with the professor's chair, which she had desired for so many years and as she struggled with disciplinary belonging. Her academic writing was a social justice project beyond disciplines, an attempt to transform academic social work to a critical and humanist-oriented discipline. She saw herself as part of a community of dissident water writers that slowly but consistently changed the conditions of research and knowledge. There was also water in the poetry lines of the previous novellas. Love and tears. She was a mother of three sons with three different surnames. This condition of the family challenged the notion of family even in a society where nuclear family was not the lived norm. Writing water was a form of organised family resistance in a society where schools forced boys to become men under pressure of symbolic and physical violence. Xenophobia and homophobia in the most equal country in the world.

* * *

Writing water builds on a series of revisits and begins with going back to the book with water in the title and to revisit a terrible series of rapes in the city, Haga, where she lived. This is where she gets stuck with the analysis for years.

One Sunday morning in December, when the landscape is covered by a thin layer of powdery snow and the kitchen smells from newly brewed coffee, the phone rings. She is surprised to hear the voice of a man who introduces himself as a journalist. He tells her that during the night between Saturday and Sunday, a woman has been raped. A snapshot of a snowy landscape and a wounded woman's body appears before her, and all she can think of is the coldness rising from the frozen ground outdoors. Next morning she gets up early and reads the headlines in the newspaper: "Violent rape. The woman fought for her life". A photograph is taken of the place of crime. A blue and white ribbon with the text "POLICE CLOSED AREA" marks that the place is a crime scene. A thin white cover of snow is lying on the ground. The colour of red, blood can be seen, and beyond this, she can see the bridge and the river partly covered with ice. The surface of the water, which still dominates the river, reflects a black shady area. According to the article, the offender attempted to kill the woman by drowning her. She fights back and lives.

Six years later, in November 2011 when I am writing this novella, I have a guest researcher position at Stockholm University and I return to the Haga case and newspaper material to study how media portrays alcohol as an explanation to rape. At the same time, in November 2011, I am invited to participate in a committee for a doctoral dissertation that studied the long-term consequences of gendered fear due to the Haga rapes. This invitation takes me back to a city that had been my home town for more than a decade, further north to water, snow and ice. I find a photo of a snow footprint of Hagaman in one of the newspapers. It evokes memories of snow angels I made both as a child and as a researcher (Livholts, 2010b). The footprint marks a time-bound figure of threatening masculinity.

>
> White on white.
> Dissolvable by time.

* * *

She leaned against the doorway. The warm palm of her hand rested against the smooth cool surface of wooden material.

It was a good spot for watching.

The red colour of the textile, which caressed along the outlines of the contours of the furniture, was attractive to the gaze.

> Expensive cover; long, high back; comfortable; easy to tilt.
> Expensive cover.
> Long, high back.
> Comfortable.
> Easy to tilt.
> Professor's Chair.

Another revisit concerns the dissolvability of the professor's chair as a career and as a structure of the power of privileged mainstream knowledge produced mainly by white men and mainstream research. The woman steals the unwanted chair, brings it to her house, and places it in her bedroom, which is also her working space. The story has a somewhat uncertain and frightening ending. Just when the woman academic think that she has escaped the white academic corridors and all the dead, unwanted, unnoticed women walking through them the last hundred years, she discovers that the walls of the new university buildings where she works are painted yellow (Gilman ([1892] 1989) and she is haunted by terrible nightmares. She begins to live through the different stories created in life and writing and dreams.

3rd April, 2011

Dear Diary,

Early spring. The ice has melted and the water cautiously begins to try out its movements. Usually I can relate my mood to the rhythm of the water, bond with the language of shifting colors, stillness, mirroring trees and stones, the shape of waves. Tonight the blank surface appears as an image of resistance that does not want to share my worries. Instead it appears as restful, promising stillness for humans who struggle. I have serious hesitations about the professor's chair. Why, one may ask, when I am so close to a much desired goal? (The reviews of my application are expected to arrive at the end of the next month.) In a week's time I am going to Edinburgh to present the third untimely academic novella in my trilogy. I realize I have been writing novellas over a period of ten years, which have actually led to creating a life story rather than just documenting it. Writing the novellas has, over time, infused an untimely element into my life. The writing and the text accompany me when I walk the streets of this small city, which I often do. I feel that my life is shaped by the existence of the novella, as if I am both that woman in the text striving for the chair, and at the same time watching this story, wanting to get out.

* * *

She is lying on the frozen ground, embraced by soft,
dry, powdery snow.
Face touches sky.
Arms and legs spread out.
The language of folding cloth marks a temporal figure.
Carefully rise to upstanding position,
Hold balance and step out of the imprint,
Watch the contours of a Snow Angel.

Snow beneath her jacket; a miniature stream of water is running down her neck. Changing form and silently disappearing.

Another return visit places the reader in the context of the snow angel, which marks a temporary figure, one important in childhood memories, and explores the emotional belonging of homeliness for the untimely academic author. In the second untimely academic novella, the author lives and works at a new university in rural space (Livholts 2010b). She is promoted to associate professor in social work and as an experimental auto/biographical project she invents 'snow angel writing' in order to trace the temporal image of embodiedness. The main characters of the story are three generations of women, she, her mother, and her maternal and paternal grandmothers.

> A large woman eating on a small plate.
> A handicraft artist, married three times and six children.
> A child in a box,
> and a child as tiny as a bag of flour.

2nd March, 2010

Dear Diary,

I am working with an interview manuscript for a publicly staged dialogue with a researcher in gender studies and reading about masculinities, gender and power. I am so engrossed in the reading that I need to rest in between chapters and articles. As I read these texts I think about the lives of me and my sons, about our movements and my work in keeping the family together by sustaining us in a web of relations, work which is ongoing even as I write this diary. Living with sons has reinforced my commitment to social justice in a society where boys become men under pressure of symbolic and physical violence.

I can see him as if it were today. Standing there beside the car, waiting for me to come and drive him to the train station. It was one of our weekends together, one of his visits. He was surprised that it was raining and looked up only to see blue sky. It was however the effect of the wind and the lake which threw rain at our faces. He looked surprised. He was soon leaving with the train and I missed him already. Every time he came to visit he would send a text message to say how far away he was at a particular moment. Every time he left he would send a text to say that he misses me already.

> In the age of speechlessness.
> A letter arrives.
> Untimely message.
> Dear Mother,
> Cannot come, so sorry.

* * *

18th September, 2011

Dear Diary,

I have been thinking about writing all day. When I woke up I was already writing, when I washed my face and looked at my greying soft thin hair I wanted to transform the mindful swirl of words to a text, a comfort zone.

Putting the kettle on, going down all the forty stairs to the post box to get the newspaper, making coffee and a sandwich. Strong autumn winds, an exhibition in the old town with my Australian friends, lunch and then no energy left. I head on home. Train, glass images of people on the move, mirroring their selves. A phone call. I reject the clearness of something that appears as a dream. I sit on my oriental carpet when I talk. Glints of my life pass. Memories, images of us. I cannot say this, I listen to him talking about his struggle. I know how hard it is. A recurring memory is that I am lying on the bed in my room in our house in the countryside. I lie there and watch the movements of a fly on the wallpaper, fascinated by its composition and liveliness. I am relieved that the wallpaper in my room is green, not yellow. But I clearly remember it had a grid pattern, which I could look at for hours.

Once, when she thought she had written, she found her body surrounded by greyish blue, the bluest grey of all colours. She is standing on the soft grass in the morning light, looking at the brownish landscape of stones.

Blank, mirroring, image of the rural.
Transparency, reflecting my future self.

Waves,
Woes,
Hope.

The rhythm of water.
Reflecting the sky, and images of forest landscape,
The place of the author.
Blackish, bluish, greyish and all the uncountable colours in between,
Depth of the unseen. Shady, in layers,
A surface of a reflective glance.

19th August, 2011

Dear Diary,

Yesterday something unexpected happened. I received the first of three reviews for the professor's chair. It was wonderful reading(!) and the summary said: "Mona Livholts merits for the professorship are obvious." And "...whose research is highly original and crosses over the boundaries of existing disciplinary borders, though escaping the research formulations typical for social work." Tears ran down my face and made the table and my clothes wet as I read it. At the same time a surge of energy that I have not felt in a long time occurred. I got up, put on my running shoes and went out. I ran to the water, at the edge of the landscape, and lay down on the warm stones. I felt my heart beating, my legs aching and the warmth from the stones. I floated away with the sound of the water and felt calmness, or nothingness or whatever one may call it. I am now waiting for the other two male professors and their reviews. I am not sure why their separate rankings have not arrived but I am afraid that the delay may bring bad news.

29th October, 2011

Dear Diary,

This week I received the other two reviewer's judgements. The two male professors gave me very positive words on several points, but they said I did not publish enough and that I could not qualify as professor in social work because what I do is too different from what social work is seen to be. I am so disappointed and overwhelmed by the power of the structures to enforce conformity to them. I began to read investigations about the situation of women professors in Scandinavian academia and learned that social work is the worst possible discipline in the social sciences if you are a woman and want to become professor. Statistics show that during the 12 year period after getting a PhD dissertation 24 percent of men and 3 percent of women become full professors. As had happened before, the statistics made me very energy less and I felt I needed to sleep for a very long time. However, I sat down that night and wrote a letter to the committee which takes the decision about future professors, arguing my qualifications for the professor's chair. Then I fell asleep.

12th November, 2011

Dear Diary,

It is a foggy day. I have lots of things to do at home but before darkness I hope I can walk to the water. The university promotions committee at Mid Sweden University decided that I am not qualified for the professor's chair in social work. They support their decision on the basis of the reviewers' judgements and take no notice of the letter I wrote. I am now waiting for the written protocol from the meeting so I can complain about the decision. Meanwhile I sent in an application for promotion to be a professor. I have heard from other Swedish academics that if you do not apply for a chair you are more likely to be promoted to professor.

I have also applied for other jobs. I applied for one job in ethnology and the reviewers said that my work is very interesting but I do not qualify as a scholar in ethnology. They thought my work is cultural sociology and literary creative writing. It seems like my qualifications do not fit into any disciplinary structure! I have also applied for a job at the school of art in Stockholm and I am now waiting to see how they will look upon my merits. The forthcoming week I will send the chapter "Writing Water" to the editor. When I signed up to write the chapter I must admit I expected that by the time I finished the novella I would have got the professor's chair. Now it seems like the future is open for several possible endings.

* * *

"The judgement of qualifications for social work are not arbitrary and do not have different application in different universities. A reasonable demand is that research should be about or be based in social work and related to social work practice, organisation and profession in relation to vulnerable people's life conditions and the structures that creates social problems/phenomena." (Reviewer)

"Let me at once underline that Livholts has a somewhat unusual research profile as a scholar in social work... to an increasing extent she has moved to a humanistic social science and general intellectual position through her increasing interest in academic writing as such... this distancing from social work becomes a dilemma when applying to become a professor in social work... despite a number of merits Livholts cannot be considered qualified for the professor's chair..." (Reviewer)

* * *

In the age of untimeliness, I was always writing water.
For the love of my sons, I became a water writer.
With the passion to transform knowledge for social justice, I am writing water.
In the age of melting ice, floods and hurricanes and a divided world, I am writing water.
Against the power of professors' chairs and through the imprints of foot prints and snow angels, I am writing water.
For the large woman who was forced to carry her child in a box and eat on a small plate, I am writing water.

For the mother who resists the patriarchal structures of society and is forced to eat on small plates, I am writing water.

For the son who is an image writer and defends the right for boys to cry, I am writing water.

For the son who is a diary and letter writer and struggles against exclusion from society and family, I am writing water.

For the son who is a fiction writer and resists violence by not using the master's tools to bully, I am writing water.

6   Open questions and concerns to guide your own situated writing

- What is theory for you? Think about theory as something we do in different situations, contexts, and spaces; think about theory as "homework" and as mo(ve)ment as suggested in this book.
- How do you understand a politics of location and diffraction as theoretical terms useful for your own writing?
- How do you understand translations of writing as epistemology, methodology, and method? Can you apply them to some of your own work, writing, or studies in research or education?
- What is the role of language in your work? How can a politics of translation be used for situated writing? Try the translation exercise, shifting between languages as illustrated in this book.
- What is your perception of the writing self? Do you think that the first person and/or third person is a possible strategy to use in your writing? Look at the examples of how the writing self can be shaped in text and, if you find it useful, try the practice of *writingwithoutspaces.*
- What objects and items do you identify as symbolic sites, useful for doing life writing in regard to your research topic? How can you design textual and visual symbolism for your chosen objects and items?
- In this book, I make use of feminist literary fiction. How can you seek inspiration from fiction to "set the stage" for your writing? Choose a literary text, a film, a play or theatre, or a combination that you think would be fruitful for the creation of a design for a story and that contributes to inspiring you to work with a particular tone.
- What "sites" do you think are available for you to write from? Think about the possibilities and limitations for diverse forms of writing in the disciplinary and institutional or interdisciplinary contexts in which you are located. How would it be possible to transgress the boundaries of such limits and work in the tensions?

- How do you understand intersecting relations of power in your writing? How can you write from the intersections that are most important in your current work? Identify visible and invisible dimensions of power and think about what genres of writing could be useful to bring them into your work.
- Choose two or more of the life writing genres in Chapter 2 (diaries, letters, memory work poetry, photography) and think about how they may be useful as a theory and method in your own situated writing.
- Look at the possibilities of using visual symbolism and/or photography. What are your perceptions of the empowering and disempowering aspects of images and photographs? Think about how you can combine visual symbolism/photography with a particular form of writing.
- Think about and discuss: what ethical questions are actualised in your writing? Write down your memories of previous situations involving ethical concerns in research, education and life, and reflect upon how you solved them.
- What aspects would you highlight if you were to define what sustainable writing at the university today and in the future is or could be?

References

Ahmed, Sara (2017) *Living a Feminist Life*. Durham, NC, and London: Duke University Press.

Andrews, Molly, Squire, Corinne & Tamboukou, Maria (2009) *Doing Narrative Research*. London: Sage.

Anzaldúa, Gloria (1987) *Borderlands/La Frontera: The New Mestiza*. San Francisco: aunt lute books. (Fourth Edition).

Barad, Karen (2014) Diffracting Diffraction: Cutting Together-Apart. *Parallax* 20(3): 168–187. DOI: 10.1080/13534645.2014.927623.

Barber, Randy, Blake, Vic, Hearn, Jeff, Jackson, David, Johnson, Richard, Luczynski, Zbyszek & McEwan, Dan (2016) *Men's Stories for a Change: Ageing Men Remember. The Older Men's Memory Work Group*. Champaign, IL: Common Ground Publishing.

Berg, Anne-Jorunn (2008) Silence and Articulation: Whiteness, Racialization and Feminist Memory Work. *NORA: Nordic Journal of Feminist and Gender Research* 16(4): 213–227.

Berger, John (1972) *Ways of Seeing*. London: Penguin.

Berger, John (1984/2005) *And Our Faces, My Heart, Brief as Photos*. London: Bloomsbury.

Berger, John & Mohr, Jean (1982/2016) *Another Way of Telling*. New York, NY: Vintage.

Bondestam, Fredrik & Lundqvist, Maja (2018) *Sexuella trakasserier i akademin. En internationell forskningsöversikt*. [Sexual Harassment in Academia. An International Research Overview]. Vetenskapsrådet.

Brah, Avtar and Phoenix, Ann (2004) Ain't I a Woman? Revisiting Intersectionality. *Journal of International Women's Studies* 5(3), 75–86. Available at: https://vc.bridgew.edu/jiws/vol5/iss3/8

Braidotti, Rosi (1994) *Nomadic Subjects: Embodiment and Sexual Difference in Contemporary Feminist Theory*. New York, NY: Columbia University Press.

Bränström Öhman, Anneli (2010) bell hooks and the Sustainability of Style. *NORA: Nordic Journal of Feminist and Gender Research* 18(4): 284–289.

Bränström Öhman, Anneli & Livholts, Mona (2007) (Eds.) *Genus och det akademiska skrivandets former*. Lund: Studentlitteratur.

Bryant, Lia & Livholts, Mona (2007) Exploring the Gendering of Space by Using Memory Work as a Reflexive Research Method. *International Journal of Qualitative Methods* 6(3): 29–43.

Bryant, Lia & Livholts, Mona (2014) Memory Work and Reflexive Gendered Bodies: Examining Rural Landscapes in the Making. In: Pini, Barbara, Brandth, Berit & Little, Jo (Eds.), *Feminisms and Ruralities*. Maryland, MD: Lexington Books, pp. 181–195.

Cixous, Hèléne (2004) Enter the Theatre. In: Prenowitz, E. (Ed.), *Selected Plays of Hélène Cixous*. London & New York, NY: Routledge, pp. 25–34.

Connell, Raewyn (2009) *Gender in World Perspective*. Cambridge: Polity.

Coylar, Julia (2009) Becoming Writing, Becoming Writers. *Qualitative Inquiry* 15(2): 421–426.

Crawford, June, Kippax, Susan, Onyx, Jenny, Gault, Una & Benton, Pam (1992) *Emotion and Gender: Constructing Meaning from Memory*. London: Sage.

Cuesta, Marta & Mulinari, Diana (2018) The Bodies of Others in Swedish Feminism. *Gender, Place & Culture*. DOI: 10.1080/0966369X.2018.1435510.

Dahl, Ulrika (2012) The Road to Writing: An Ethno(Bio)Graphic Memoir. In: Livholts, Mona (Ed.) *Emergent Writing Methodologies in Feminist Studies*. London and New York, NY: Routledge, pp. 148–165.

Davies, Bronwyn & Gannon, Susanne (2006). (Eds.) *Doing Collective Biography: Investigating the Production of Subjectivity*. New York, NY: Open University Press.

Ehrnberger, Karin (2017) *Tillblivelser. En trasslig berättelse om design som normkritisk praktik*. Doktorsavhandling i maskinkonstruktion, inriktning produkt- och servicedesign. [Becomings. An Entangled Narrative about Design as Norm Critical Practice]. Kungliga tekniska högskolan, Stockholm.

Ellis, Carolyn (2007) Telling Secrets, Revealing Lives: Relational Ethics in Research with Intimate Others. *Qualitative Inquiry* 13(1): 3–29.

Eng, Heidi (2012) Sensitive Studies, Sensitive Writings: Poetic Tales of Sexuality in Sport. In: Livholts, Mona (Ed.) *Emergent Writing Methodologies in Feminist Studies*. London: Routledge, pp. 166–177.

Farahani, Fataneh (2014) Hem, hemlöshet och allt däremellan. Rutten från en obekvämhet till en annan. [Home, Homelessness and Everything in Between]. In: Lundberg, Anna & Werner, Ann (Eds.). *Kreativt skrivande och kritiskt tänkande i genusvetenskap*. [Creative Writing and Critical Thinking in Gender Studies]. Rapport, Nationella genussekretariatet för genusforskning: 25–34. https://www.genus.se/wp-content/uploads/Kreativt-skrivande-och-kritisk-tankande-i-genusvetenskap.pdf

Frankenberg, Ruth (1993) *White Women, Race Matters: The Social Construction of Whiteness*. Minneapolis: University of Minnesota Press.

Gannon, Susanne (2012) From the Curve of the Snake and the Scene of the Crocodile: Musings on Learning and Losing Space, Place and Body. *Reconceptualising Educational Research Methodology* 3(2): 7–15.

Gilman, Charlotte Perkins (1892/1989). *The Yellow Wallpaper and Other Writings*. New York, NY: Bentam books.

Gordon, Sindi Fiona (2015) *Krik? Krak! Exploring the Potential of Creative Life Writing for Opening Dialogic Space and Increasing Personal Freedom.* Doctoral thesis (PhD), University of Sussex.

Grosz, Elizabeth (2010) The Untimeliness of Feminist Theory. *NORA: Nordic Journal of Feminist and Gender Studies* 18(1): 48–51.

Gunaratnam, Yasmin (2011) Cultural Vulnerability: A Narrative Approach to Intercultural Care. *Qualitative Social Work* 12(2): 104–118.

Halldorsdottir, Erla Hulda, Hyvärinen, Matti, Israel, Kali, Jackson Stevi, Mitzal, Barbara A., Salter, Andrea, Stanley, Liz, & Tamboukou, Maria (2010) Commentaries on the Professor's Chair. *Life Writing* (7)2: 169–172.

Hallgren, Hanna (2006) Det transversala språket / Att förnimma världen. [The Transversal Language / About Percieving the World]. *Nypoesi* 2/6. https://nypoesi.net/tidsskrift/206/?tekst=13

Hallgren, Hanna (2015) Writing as a Method: A Study in Poetry, Writing Process and the Possibilities of Reflexive Academic Writing. *From Arts College to University: Artistic Research Yearbook 2015*: 76–89. Retrieved 2018-08-10 at: https://publikationer.vr.se/produkt/arsbok-kfou-2015-fran-konstnarlig-hogskola-till-universitet/

Hallgren, Hanna (2017) The I/Eye Is in the Verb: Towards a Poetics of the Feminist Poetic I *HumaNetten* 38: 109–114.

Hau'ofa, Epeli (2008) *We Are the Ocean: Selected Works.* Honolulu: University of Hawaii Press.

Haraway, Donna (1988) Situated Knowledges: The Science Question in Feminism and the Privilege of Partial Perspective. *Feminist Studies* 14(3): 575–599.

Haraway, Donna (2000) *How Like a Leaf: An Interview with Thyrza Nichols Goodeve.* New York, NY: Routledge.

Harding, Sandra (1987) Instabiliteten i den feministiska teoribildningens analytiska kategorier. [The Instability in the Analytical Categories of Feminist Theory]. *Kvinnovetenskaplig tidskrift* 2–3: 4–35.

Haug, Frigga (2008) Memory-Work as a Method of Social Science Research: A Detailed Rendering of Memory-Work Method. In: Hyle, Adrienne. E., Ewing, Margaret S., Montgomery, Diane, and Kaufman, Judith S (Eds.), *Dissecting the Mundane: International Perspectives on Memory-Work.* Lanham, MD: University Press of America, pp. 21–41.

Haug, Frigga and Others (1987) *Female Sexualization: A Collective Work of Memory.* London: Verso.

Herman, David (2002) *Story Logic: Problems and Possibilities of Narrative.* Lincoln, Nebraska: University of Nebraska Press.

hooks, bell (1989) *Talking Back: Thinking Feminist, Thinking Black.* Boston, MA: South End Press.

hooks, bell (1997) *Wounds of Passion: A Writing Life.* New York, NY: Henry Holt Company.

hooks, bell (1999) *Remembered Rapture: The Writer at Work.* London: The Women's Press.

Holmquist, Anna (2019) The Production Novella as a Textual and Visual Narrative Methodology in Craft-Based Design and Artistic Research. In:

Almevik, Gunnar & Westin, Jonathan (Eds.), *Craft Sciences*. Acta Universitatis Gothoburgensis, Studies in Conservation, Gothenburg University. In press.

Hyle, Adrienne E., Ewing, Margaret S., Montgomery, Diane & Kaufman, Judith S. (2008) *Dissecting the Mundane: International Perspectives on Memory-Work*. Lanham, MD: University Press of America.

Hyvärinen, Matti (2008) Analyzing Narratives and Story-Telling. In Alasuutari, Pertti, Bickman, Leonard & Brannen, Julia (Eds.) *The SAGE Handbook of Social Research Methods*. London: Sage, pp. 447–460.

Jolly, Margaretta (2001) *Encyclopedia of Life Writing: Autobiographical and Biographical Forms*. Chicago, IL: Fitzroy Dearborn.

Jolly, Margaretta (2011) Life Writing as Critical Creative Practice. *Literature Compass*, 8(12): 878–889.

Jolly, Margaretta & Stanley, Liz (2005) Letters As / Not a Genre. *Life Writing*, 1(2): 1–18.

Jones, Kathleen B. (2012) Masquerades of Love: Biographical and Autobiographical Explorations of Self-Invention with/in Hanna Arendt's Rahel Varnhagen. In: Livholts, Mona (Eds.) *Emergent Writing Methodologies in Feminist Studies*. London: Routledge, pp. 55–70.

Jones, Kathleen B. (2013) *Diving for Pearls: A Thinking Journey with Hanna Arendt*. San Diego, CA: Thinking Women Books.

Keen, Martha (2016) Life Writing and the Empathetic Circle. *Concentric: Literary and Cultural Studies* September: 9–26. DOI: 10.6240/concentric. lit.2016.42.2.02.

Kelly, John Farell & Livholts, Mona (2014) Light on Water: Conversations on Emergent Writing Methodologies. *Writers in Conversation*. 1(2) August. http:// dspace.flinders.edu.au/jspui/bitstream/2328/27829/1/Livholts_Kelly.pdf

King, Stephen (2000) *On Writing: A Memoir of the Craft*. New York, NY: Scribner.

Kuhn, Anette (1995) *Family Secrets: Acts of Memory and Imagination*. London and New York, NY: Verso Classics.

Kuhn, Anette (2010) Memory Texts and Memory Work: Performances of Memory in and with Visual Media. *Memory Studies* 3(4): 298–313.

Kuhn, Anette & Emiko McAllister, Kirsten (2006) *Locating Memory: Photographic Acts*. New York, NY: Berghahn.

Küster, Marc Wilhelm (2016) Writing Beyond the Letter. *Tijdschrift Voor Mediageschiedenis*, 19(2): 1–17.

Leavy, Patricia (2013) *Fiction as Research Practice*. Walnut Creek, CA: Left Coast Press.

Leavy, Patricia (2015) *Method Meets Art: Art-Based Research Practice*. New York, NY and London: Guilford Press. (Second edition)

Lejeune, Philippe (2009) Composing a Diary. In: Popkin, J. & Rak, J. (Eds.) *Philip Lejeune: On Diary*. Translated by K. Durnin. Honolulu: University of Hawaii Press, pp. 168–174.

Livholts, Mona (2001/2011) *"Women", Welfare, Textual Politics and Critique: An Invitation to a ThinkingWriting Methodology in the Study of Welfare*. PhD Dissertation, Saarbrucken: Lambert Academic Publishing.

Livholts, Mona (2007) Professorsstolen. [The Professor's Chair]. In: Bränström Öhman, Annelie & Livholts, Mona (Eds.). *Genus och det akademiska skrivandets former.* [Gender and Forms of Academic Writing]. Lund: Studentlitteratur, pp. 89–110.

Livholts, Mona (2008) "Det tänkandeskrivande subjektet. Reflektioner kring metodologiska postulat, svensk genusforskning och post/akademiskt skrivande" [The ThinkingWriting Subject. Reflections on Methodological Postulates, Swedish Gender Research and Post/Academic Writing]. *Tidskrift för Genusvetenskap* 2: 283–298.

Livholts, Mona (2009) "To Theorise in a More Passionate Way." Carol Lee Bacchi's Diary of Mothering and Contemporary Post/Academic Writing Strategies. *Feminist Theory* 10(1): 121–131.

Livholts, Mona (2010a) The Professor's Chair: An Untimely Academic Novella. *Life Writing* 7(2): 155–168.

Livholts, Mona (2010b) The Snow Angel and Other Imprints: An Untimely Academic Novella. *International Review of Qualitative Research* 3(1): 103–124.

Livholts, Mona (2010c) Writing Masculinities, Gender and the Politics of Change: A Publicly Staged Interview with Raewyn Connell. *NORA: Nordic Journal of Feminist and Gender Research* 18(2): 246–266.

Livholts, Mona (2012a) (Ed.) *Emergent Writing Methodologies in Feminist Studies.* New York, NY, and London: Routledge.

Livholts, Mona (2012b) "To Fill Academic Work with Political Passion": Nina Lykke's Cosmodolphins and Contemporary Post/Academic Writing Strategies. *Feminist Review* 102: 135–142.

Livholts, Mona (2013) Writing Water: An Untimely Academic Novella. In: Stanley, Liz (Ed.), *Documents of Life Revisited: Narrative and Biographical Methods for a 21st Century of Critical Humanism.* Farnham: Ashgate, pp. 177–192.

Livholts, Mona (2015a) A Politics of Location in Discourse and Narrative Studies. In: Livholts, Mona & Tamboukou, Maria, *Discourse and Narrative Methods: Theoretical Departures, Analytical Strategies and Situated Writing.* London: Sage, pp. 137–148.

Livholts, Mona (2015b) Working with Memories and Images. In: Livholts, Mona & Tamboukou, Maria, *Discourse and Narrative Methods: Theoretical Departures, Analytical Strategies and Situated Writing.* London: Sage, pp. 162–176.

Livholts, Mona (2015c) Untimely Academic Novella Writing. In: Livholts, Mona & Tamboukou, Maria, *Discourse and Narrative Methods: Theoretical Departures, Analytical Strategies and Situated Writing.* London: Sage, pp. 177–191.

Livholts, Mona (2015d) Imagine Transfiguration. The chapter exhibition as a critical and creative space for knowledge in social work and media studies. In Bryant L. (Ed.) *Critical and Creative Qualitative Research Methodologies for Social Work.* Farnham: Ashgate, pp. 131–158.

Livholts, Mona (2016a) Permission for Untimely Writing. In: White, Julie (Ed.), *Permission: The International Interdisciplinary Impact of Laurel Richardson's Work.* Rotterdam: Sense Publishers, pp. 144–146.

Livholts, Mona (2016b) Writing, Telling, Listening, Reading, Seeing: The Creative Use of Self in Research by Working with Memories and Images. *The Psychotherapist, UKCP's Magazine*: UK Council for Psychotherapy: 25–27.

Livholts, Mona (2017) "What We Learn How to See": A Politics of Location and Situated Knowledge in Glocal Social Work. In Livholts, M. & Bryant, L. (Eds.), *Social Work in a Glocalised World*. London: Routledge, pp. 89–105.

Livholts, Mona (2018) Narrative Writing as Art Based Practice. *Synnyt/Origins: Finnish Studies in Art Education*, 3: 9–30.

Livholts, Mona & Bryant, Lia (2013) Gender and the Telephone: Voice and Emotions Shaping and Gendering Space. *Human Technology: An Interdisciplinary Journal on Humans in ICT Environments*, 9(2), 157–170.

Livholts, Mona & Tamboukou, Maria (2015) *Discourse and Narrative Methods: Theoretical Departures, Analytical Strategies and Situated Writing*. London: Sage.

Lorde, Audre (1984) *Sister Outsider: Essays and Speeches by Audre Lorde*. Marshall: The Crossing Press Feminist Series; Freedom, CA: The Crossing Press.

Lorde, Audre (1997) *The Collected Poems of Audre Lorde*. New York, NY and London: W. W. Norton and Company.

Lykke, Nina (2014) (Ed.) *Writing Academic Texts Differently: Intersectional Feminist Methodologies and the Playful Art of Writing*. London: Routledge.

McCulliss Debbie (2013) Poetic Inquiry and Multidisciplinary Qualitative Research. *Journal of Poetry Therapy* 26(2): 83–114. DOI: 10.1080/08893675. 2013.794536.

McNeill, L. (2005) Editorial: Labeling Ourselves: Genres and Life Writing. *Life Writing* 2(2): 7–18.

Minh-Ha, Trinh (1989) *Woman, Native, Other: Writing Postcoloniality and Feminism*. New York, NY: Routledge.

Mohanty, Chandra Talpade (2003) *Feminism without Borders: Decolonising Theory, Practicing Solidarity*. Durham, NC: Duke University Press.

Moi, Toril (2008) "I am not a Woman Writer". About Women, Literature and Feminist Theory. *Feminist Theory*, 9(3): 259–271. DOI: 10.1177/1464700108095850.

Nobel, Andreas (2014) *Dimmer på upplysningen – text, form och formgivning*. Akademisk avhandling, 2014:1: KTH, Arkitekturskolan och konstfack: Stockholm.

Nowotny, Helga (2008) The Potential of Transdisciplinarity. *Interdisciplines*, 7: 1–4. Accessed 2018-08-10: http://www.helga-nowotny.eu/downloads/helga_nowotny_b59.pdf

Oakley, Ann (2010) The Social Science of Biographical Life-Writing: Some Methodological and Ethical Issues. *International Journal of Social Research Methodology* 13(5): 425–439. DOI: 10.1080/13645571003593583.

Orwell, George (1946/2004) *Why I Write*. London: Penguin.

Page, Tiffany (2017) Vulnerable Writing as a Feminist Methodological Practice. *Feminist Review* 115(1): 13–29.

Pease, Bob (2008) Mothers and Sons: Using Memory Work to Explore the Subjectivities and Practices of Profeminist Men. In Hyle, Adrienne E., Ewing, Margaret S., Montgomery, Diane & Kaufman, Judith S. (Eds.) *Dissecting the Mundane: International Perspectives on Memory-Work*. Lanham, MD: University Press of America, pp. 133–150.

Pease, Bob (2010) *Undoing Privilege: Unearned Advantage in a Divided World*, London: Zed.

Piper, Adrian (1993) *Ethics of Change: Women in the 90s: Sex, Power and Politics*. Atlantic Centre for the Arts, New Smyrna Beach, FL.

Plummer, Ken (2001) *Documents of Life 2: An Invitation to a Critical Humanism*. London: Sage. (Second edition).

Plummer, Ken (2013) A Manifesto for Social Stories. In: Stanley, Liz (Ed.), *Documents of Life Revisited: Narrative and Biographical Methodology for a 21st Century Critical Humanism*. Farnham: Ashgate, pp. 209–219.

Rendell, Jane (2001) *Walking to Wapping/Walking with Angels*, collected 2018-08-12 at: http://www.janerendell.co.uk/wp-content/uploads/2009/03/wappingangels.pdf

Rendell, Jane (2010) *Site-Writing: The Architecture of Art Criticism*. London and New York, NY: I.B. Tauris.

Richardson, Laurel (1994) Writing: A Method of Inquiry. In: Denzin, N. K. & Lincoln, Y. S. (Eds.), *Handbook of Qualitative Research*. London: Sage.

Richardson, Laurel (1997) *Fields of Play. Constructing an Academic Life*. New Brunswick, NJ: Rutgers University Press.

Riessman, Catherine K. (2008) *Narrative Methods in the Human Sciences*. London: Sage.

Scott, K. (2018) *Seeking Middle-Classness: University Students in Iraqi Kurdistan*. Dissertation, Faculty of Social Sciences, Department of Gender Studies. Lund: Lund University.

Sohl, Lena (2014) *Att veta sin klass. Kvinnors uppåtgående klassresor i Sverige*. [Knowing Your Class. The Upward Class Travelling of Women in Sweden]. Stockholm: Atlas bokförlag.

Sontag, Susan (2007) The Image World. In Evans Jessica & Hall Stuart (Eds). *Visual Culture. The Reader*. London: Sage, pp. 80–94.

Spivak, Gayatri Chakravorty (1993) The Politics of Translation. In: Spivak, Gayatri Chakravorti (Ed.), *Outside in the Teaching Machine*. New York, NY: Routledge, pp. 179–200.

Stanley, Liz (1995) *The Auto/Biographical/I: Theory and Practice of Feminist Auto/Biography*. Manchester: Manchester University Press.

Stanley, Liz (2004) The Epistolarium: On Theorizing Letters and Correspondences. *Auto/Biography* 12(3): 201–235.

Stanley, Liz (2013) Introduction: Documents of Life and Critical Humanism in Narrative and Biographical Frame. In: Stanley, Liz (Ed.), *Documents of Life Revisited: Narrative and Biographical Methodology for a 21st Century Critical Humanism*. Farnham: Ashgate, pp. 3–16.

Stanley, Liz (2015) The Death of the Letter, Epistolary Intent, Letterness, and the Many Ends of Letter Writing. *Cultural Sociology* 9(2): 240–255.

Stanley, Liz & Jolly, Margaretta (2017) Epistolarity: Life after Death of the Letter? *a/b: Auto/Biography Studies* 32(2): 229–233: DOI: 10.1080/08989575. 2016.1187040.

Stanley, Liz & Wise, Susan (2000) But the Empress Has No Clothes! Some Awkward Questions about the "Missing Revolution". *Feminist Theory* 1(3): 261–288.

Stein, Gertrude (1931/1975) *How to Write*. New York, NY: Dover Publications.

Tamboukou, Maria (2015a) Working with Diaries and Letters. In: Livholts, M & Tamboukou, M (Eds.), *Discourse and Narrative Methods: Theoretical Departures, Analytical Strategies and Situated Writing*. London: Sage, pp. 149–161.

Tamboukou, Maria (2015b) Farewell to the Self: Between the Letter and the Self-Portrait. *Life Writing* 12(1): 75–91. DOI: 10.1080/14484528.2013.810242.

Tamboukou, Maria (2018) Rethinking the Subject in Feminist Research: Narrative Personae and Stories of "The Real". *Textual Practice*: 939–955. DOI: 10.1080/0950236X.2018.1486541.

Ulmer, Jasmine B. (2017) Writing Slow Ontology. *Qualitative Inquiry* 23(3): 201–211.

Ulmer, Jasmine B. (2018) Minor Gestures: Slow Writing and Everyday Photography, *Qualitative Research in Psychology* 15(2–3): 317–322. DOI: 10.1080/14780887.2018.1430016.

Warren, John & Kilgard, Amy (2001) Staging Stain upon the Snow: Performance as a Critical Enfleshment of Whiteness. *Text and Performance Quarterly* 21(4): 261–264.

Widerberg, Karin (2010) In the Homes of Others: Exploring New Sites and Methods when Investigating the Doings of Gender, Class and Ethnicity. *Sociology* 44(6): 1181–1196.

Widerberg, Karin (2016) Explorative Teaching and Research: From Memory Work to Experience Stories. *Creative Education* 7: 1935–1952.

Williams, Patricia (1991) *The Alchemy of Race and Rights: The Diary of a Law Professor*. Cambridge, MA: Harvard University Press.

Witkin, Stanley L. (2014) *Narrating Social Work through Autoethnography*. New York, NY: Columbia University Press.

Witkin, Stanley L. & Chambon, Adrienne (2007) New Voices in Social Work: Writing Forms and Knowledge Production, *Qualitative Social Work* 6(4): 387–395.

Woolf, Virginia (1929) A *Room of One's Own*. New York, NY: Harcourt, Brace and Company.

Wyatt, Jonathan, Gale, Ken, Gannon, Susan & Davies, Bronwyn (2011) *Deleuze & Collaborative Writing: An Immanent Plane of Composition*. New York, NY: Peter Lang.

Yuval-Davis, Nira (2015) Situated Intersectionality and Social Inequality. *Raisons Politiques*, 58: 91–100.

Zarkov, Dubravka & Davies, Kathy (2018) Ambiguities and Dilemmas around #MeToo: #ForHow Long and #WhereTo? *European Journal of Women's Studies* 25(1): 3–9.

Index